T0057355

THE DEVIL'S PANTIES

Volume
2
by Jennie Breeden

ARCHAIA STUDIOS PRESS

The Devil's Panties
Volume 2
Written & Illustrated
by Jennie Breeden

Published by
Archaia Studios Press
586 Devon Street, 3rd Floor
Kearny, NJ 07032
www.aspcomics.com

Mark Smylie & Aki Liao, *Publishers*
Joseph Illidge, *Comics Editor*
Pauline Beney, *Art Director*
Brian Petkash & Lys Fulda, *Marketing*

Write to:
editorial@aspcomics.com

The Devil's Panties Volume 2
July 2008
FIRST PRINTING
10 9 8 7 6 5 4 3 2 1

ISBN 1-932386-36-X
ISBN 13: 978-1-932386-36-3

Printed in Hong Kong.

OK, GUYS, PUBLIC SERVICE ANNOUNCEMENT

DO **NOT** CALL A GIRL "SWEETIE," "SUGAR," "HONEY," "BABY" OR **TOOTS**

AND STAY AWAY FROM "MA'AM" OR "YOUNG LADY" TOO.

WHAT **CAN** WE CALL YOU?

UM.... BOO BOO KITTY FUCK*?

WARNING
IF SOMEONE WITH A DICK THAT **WASN'T** KEVIN SMITH **DID** SAY THIS TO A WOMAN, THEN HE'D PROBABLY FIND HIMSELF **WITHOUT** SAID DICK.

*JAY AND SILENT BOB STRIKE BACK

WHAT NEVER TO SAY IN THE BEDROOM

DOES YOUR MOM LIKE ME?

HUFF! PANT!

WHEEZE! HACK!

GHASP! CHOKE.

THIS **WHEEZE!** IS SUPPOSED **COUGH!** TO BE HEALTHY!?

SOB!

PANT!

I DON'T WANNA SEE "BLAZING SADDLES" AGAIN.

WHERE ALL THE WHITE WOMEN AT?

PUT IN "MILO AND OTIS".

CLICKCLICK

VOLUME ||||||||||||||...

...ELL INTO THE RIVER HOW WELL... DIES

BARK BARK

MEW

MOO

MEW MEW

BARK LEAVE

SADIST!

SO WHAT KINDA ANIME DO YOU WATCH?

MY FIRST ANIME WAS RANMA, BUT I REALLY LIKE COWBOY BEBOP AN ESCAFLOWNE.

SO, IN OTHER WORDS, CHICK STUFF.

DRAGON BALL Z

OH, YOU POOR BOY. OUTSIDE OF A STORM TROOPER CIRCLE JERK, YOU'RE NEVER GETTING LAID.

ICE AGE DARK

YUGI YUGI

YUGIOH

YUGIOH

THIS COMIC'S DAMAG...

DO YOU HAVE MA... ACTI... FIG #7...

DO YOU SELL BASEBALL CARDS?

I WANT ...IDERMAN #63. I WANNA KNOW HOW ...CH $ ...S WORTH.

BOSS, I'M GONNA NEED A SMOKE BREAK.

BUT YOU DON'T SMOKE.

YEAH, WELL, I DON'T KILL PEOPLE EITHER...

...BUT THERE'S A FIRST TIME FOR EVERYTHING!

STAPLE FLYERS.

KU CHUNK!

CUT CARDS.

CREAK!

SHRINK WRAP WATER COLOR PRINTS.

SSSSS

MMM BURNING PLASTIC.

SO BEGINS CONVENTION SEASON...

DID THE PRINTER EVER SEND YOU YOUR COMICS?

I DON'T CARE.

OH GOD, DRAGON CON HASN'T STARTED YET AND I ALREADY FEEL HUNG OVER!

HE'S ONLY TALKING TO YOU BECAUSE YOU HAVE BOOBS.

USE ALL YOUR ASSETS!

YOU'RE ALREADY SELLING BITS OF YOUR SOUL, MIGHT AS WELL USE YOUR BODY FOR MARKETING.

STOP SMILING! YOU'RE LEADING HIM ON!

THEY'LL BUY MORE BOOKS IF THEY THINK YOU'LL SLEEP WITH THEM

WHAT'S IN THE BAG?

NONSENSE.

GET YOUR HORNS OFF MY ASS!

TRAS

YOU NEED SATANIC PORN!

JEN, THIS IS MY LITTLE BROTHER.

BUDDY FROM COLLEGE

UM.

OH.... UH.... LOOK! MARK HAMILL!

HEY, MARK!

GHHHNNU!

GREAT ZOMBIE COS—OW!

EW!

MGRPHO NN

NH

EEW! NOW MY EAR'S GONNA BE ALL BLOODY FOR MY PANEL DISCUSSION!

OFF!

NGHHUNRUUWA!

BAD ZOMBIE!

"TAKE THE KIDS TO SEE SUPERMAN" SHE SAYS.

BRAINS.

SO ....UM...

..WHAT ARE YOU DOING LATER?

11

PPHTOO!

FUCK!

WHO PUT COFFEE IN MY RUM??

EXPLAIN TO ME AGAIN *WHY* PEOPLE ENJOY INGESTING MILD POISONS??

HEY, JEN, WANT SOME AGUA?

SURE, I COULD USE SOME HYDRATION.

SHOULD IT SMELL LIKE *BATTERY ACID?*

YES! DRINK IT!

SIP.

HACK! COUGH WHEEZE! AACK! GAG! WEE SP COUGH! COUGH! WHEEZE GASP! COUGH! ACK!

GOOD LORD, WOMAN! PASS ME THAT BOTTLE!

WHERE WE GOIN'?

FONDUE.

OH, OK.

WHEN DID I GET COVERED IN SHARPIE?

MMM. FONDUE GOOD! I WONDER WHAT KINDA DESSERTS THEY'VE GOT.

CHOCOLATE FONDUE. IT TAKES A WEEK TO MAKE AND YOU NEED RESERVATIONS JUST TO ORDER IT.

I NEED A CIGARETTE.

REMOVE
LL METAL
EMS AND
N CRATE
OCEDING
UGH
ETE

DEVILS PANTS

REMOVE SHOES

BOOT BUCKLE, NECKLACE, STUDS ON BELT OH MET FUCK IT

SUBDIVISIONS TAKING OVER THE BACK WOODS. STRIP MALLS AND ROADS EXPANDING...

...MY LITTLE HOME TOWN IS CHANGING SO MUCH.

WILL IT EVER BE THE SAME HOME THAT I REMEMBER?

SKYLER, STOP WATCHING TV AND DO YOUR CHORES! XIAN, WHERE'S MY DRILL!

HOME SWEET HOME!

YAY, SKYLER! IT'S SO GOOD TO SEE YOU SISTER, DARLING!

SO, JEN, YOU GAY YET?

DAMNIT, SKYLER! YOU'VE MET MY BOYFRIEND!

DENIAL ISN'T JUST A RIVER IN EGYPT, SISTER, DARLING!

SUMMER WANTS US TO COME BY AND VISIT HER IN PITTSBURGH ON OUR WAY TO BALTIMORE.

OK.

..... PITTSBURGH IS **NOT** "ON THE WAY" TO BALTIMORE FROM VIRGINIA

DO YOU **REALLY** WANT TO INCUR THE WRATH OF THE BABY OF THE BREEDEN CLAN??

...... GOOD POINT.

YAY! MY SISTERS ARE—

PARKING DECK

SNARLE! GROWL! RAWR

JEN'S BEEN TRAVELING FOR TWO DAYS SOLID AN SHE'S STILL A LITTLE HUNG OVER FROM DRAGON CON.

GIVE HER FIVE MINUTES TO DECOMPRESS.

OK.

DORMS.

HERE'S A FLYER FOR A PARTY TONIGHT.

IS...IS THIS A **FRAT** PARTY?

UH... YEAH?

ARE YOU...

...FRAT BOYS?

UH.

WAIT, **ONE** MORE PICTURE! STOP SQUIRMING!

I WAS GOING TO TAKE YOU GUYS TO A GAY BAR, BUT IF YOU WANNA GO TO THE FRAT PARTY INSTEAD.

HMM.

LET'S SEE.... GORGEOUS, HALF NAKED, DANCING MEN TO OGLE...

...OR DRUNKEN, OGLING, JUVENILE, UNWASHED, FRATBOYS....

...HMMM, DECISIONS, DECISIONS.

WHO KNEW THAT PITTSBURGH HAD SUCH A GREAT GAY BAR.

ON LIBERTY AVENUE......

...WAITAMINUTE, WHERE HAVE I HEARD THAT NAME?

"QUEER AS FOLK"

GASP! SQUEEL!

HEY, GUYS, THESE ARE MY SISTERS.

HEY, HON, COME DANCE WITH ME?

K.

I SUDDENLY FEEL THAT I MUST PAY YOU.

AW.

EXCUSE ME, COULD I-

DO YOU HAVE ANY-

HEEYY...

GOOD GOD, MY BOOBS HAVE NO POWER HERE.

I'M GLAD SUMMER BROUGHT US TO THIS CLUB, IT'S GREAT! WHERE'S OUR BABY SIS, ANYWAY?

SHE'S DANCING UP ON STAGE, SANDWICHED BETWEEN FOUR HALF NAKED, SWEATY GAY MEN.

AAH! IT BURNS!

HEY, SUMMER, CAN I COME WITH YOU TO YOUR MORNING CLASS?

SURE.

WELCOME TO POP CULTURE 101

TODAY WE'LL BE TALKING ABOUT REALITY TV.

AND PEOPLE THINK COMIC BOOKS* IS A FLUFF MAJOR?

*SEQUENTIAL ART YES, I MAJORED IN IT.

COMIC CON BINGO PROVIDED BY WWW.YOUNGAMERICANCOMICS.COM

MY HALLOWEEN COSTUME IS GONNA BE **SO COOL!**

I'VE GOT MY ORAN... HAIR AND PURPLE FEATHERED HAT AN... STRIPEY TIGHTS SPARK... ...WINGS AND... ...ICKS A... BRO... ...JACK... CAND... ...GLOWS... BIN... ...AKEU... GREEN... ...PA... BOOTS... NAIL... COBW... FACEP... GLOWI...

DON'T YOU NEED A DRESS OR SOMETHING?

DETAILS... DETAILS.

I'VE GOT EVERYTHING I NEED FOR MY HALLOWEEN COSTUME!

EXCEPT FOR A BLACK BALLERINA SKIRT.

CURSSESS!

SO I'M GONNA **SEW** ONE!

YOU CAN SEW?

UM.....I CAN SEW AS WELL AS I CAN COOK?

WE'RE DOOMED.

I DON'T WANNA GO TO A GROWN-UP HALLOWEEN PARTY. YOU JUST DRESS UP AN' DRINK ALL NIGHT.

I WANNA GO TRICK-OR-TREATING! ALL I NEED IS SOME KIDS..

DON'T LOOK AT ME!!

HMMM PLOT PLOT PLANSCHEME

AH **HA!** I'VE GOT AN OLDER SISTER! **SHE'S** GOT KIDS.

AND THEY'RE IN MY SAME GENE POOL, SO THE'RE KINDA IMMUNE TO ME!

BE AFRAID.

HEY, SIS! CAN I BORROW YOUR RUGRATS?

WHAT'CHA DOIN'?

FACE PAINT.

ISN'T THAT WATER COLOR PAINT?

YEAH.

I WAS GOING TO USE SPRAY PAINT, BUT THEY DIDN'T HAVE THE RIGHT SHADE OF GREEN.

THIS EXPLAINS SO MUCH.

PASS ME THAT TUBE OF OIL PAINT, WILL YOU?

HEY BIG SIS, READY FOR TRICK-OR-TREATING?

YEAH, BUT WE'RE NOT DOING ALL THAT MUCH. HON, COULD YOU TAKE THE HOT DOGS OFF THE GRILL?

CAERFUL CARVING THE PUMPKIN, HON. GO GET IN YOUR COSTUME, INVITE THE TRICK-OR-TREAT KIDS IN FOR DINNER.

SUBURBIA.

HEY, GUYS. HOW WAS YOUR DRIVE?

HEY, SIS. JUST THE SAME MIND-NUMBING, ATLANTA-TO-SAVANNAH, DESOLATE HIGHWAY.

WE'VE GOT THE GUEST ROOM READY FOR YOU.

I BROUGHT COOKIES FOR TOMORROWS THANKSGIVING DINNER.

GREAT. PUT THEM IN THE OTHER ROOM WITH THE PUMPKIN, APPLE, AND PECAN PIES, CAKE, MUFFINS, COOKIES AND FUDGE.

HURRY UP AND GO TO BED SO WE CAN WAKE UP AND EAT ALL THAT!!

HEY, JON.

HEY, JEN.

YOU KNOW LAST YEAR HOW MY SISTER WAS SO PREGNANT WE HAD TO USE A CRANE TO MOVE HER?

THIS IS WHAT CAME OUT.

GOOD GOO, THEY'RE GINORMOUS!

TWANG

WRR WRR

33

SHOPPING.

SHOPPING.

SHOPPING.

TICKTICKTICKTICKTICKTICKTI DING!

OK I'M DONE! THAT'S IT! I WANNA GO HOME NOW!

I SAVED YOU SOME DONUTS.

NGHKAY.

AND SIS WANTS YOU TO BE IN THE FAMILY PICTURE THIS YEAR.

NGKAY.

WAITAMINUTE, WHAT?

I SO HAPPY YOU TAKING FAMILY PICTURE WITH US, JEN.

YOU CAN NEVER LEAVE NOW.

OK EVERYONE, SMILE!

COME ON, BIG SMILES!

GOOD!

FLASH!

BE GOOD.

WHY?

IT'S SO GOOD YOU CAME.

YOU TAKE GOOD CARE MY BOY....

YOU HAVE BABY NOW.

HEH. HEH.

WILL YOU JUST **FALL** ALREADY!?!

37

WRITTEN BY WILLIAM CADRIN

CHILDHOOD: YOU ASK FOR WHAT YOU WANT
ADULTHOOD: YOU ASK FOR WHAT YOU NEED.

AND A LEAF BLOWER, AND A LABRIS, AND KITCHEN CHAIRS, AND A FAN BELT, AND STORM WINDOWS, AND A LADDER, AND NEW ROCKS, AND DREMEL, AND A LAZER PRINTER, AND RAINBOW BRIGHT DVD, AND STARSCREAM TRANSFORMER, AND A BATMAN UTILITY BELT.

David Mack creator of Kabuki comic book

HI, I'M DAVID MACK.

YOUR CO-WORKER SAID YOU READ MY STUFF.

THIS IS A REALLY GREAT STORE.

YOU'RE PRETTY.

I'VE SEEN YOU AT SOME CONVENTIONS.

I'M GLAD YOU LIKE MY WORK.

WOULD YOU LIKE ME TO SIGN SOMETHING?

OH MY GOD, DAVID MACK WAS IN THE STORE!

CLICK CLICK CLICK CLICK

HE'S ALL MUSCLES AN SHOULDERS AND HE GRINNED AT ME!

SO I'M GONNA BE THE WEEKEND BOYFRIEND, HUH?

GREAT! MORE TIME FOR VIDEO GAMES!

COULD WE **PLEASE** TURN THE HEAT UP?

CHATTER! *SHIVER!* *CHATTER!*

FINE! FINE...

..YOU CAN USE ONE OF MY SWEATERS.

ARE MY LITTLE SISTERS READY TO GO SALSA DANCING?

YUP!

HOLD ON, I HAVE TO GET ONE MORE THING...

WHAT'S THAT?

...BULLETS.

NO!

HEY, JEN, WELCOME TO "WHAT THE HELL?" CONVENTION.

WE'RE REALLY BIG FANS.

IF THERE'S ANYTHING YOU NEED, JUST ASK.

OKAY.

I'VE BEEN CLONED.

HEY, HON, HOW'S THE CONVENTION?

GREAT!

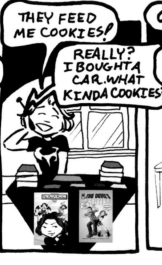

THEY FEED ME COOKIES!

REALLY? I BOUGHT A CAR. WHAT KINDA COOKIES?

OREO!

COOL, WELL HAVE FUN.

OKAY, SEE YA LATER

BYE, HON.

Likely Stories

WAIT, ... WHAT?

CAN I BID ON GUYS IN THE GEEK AUCTION?

Schedule
Croputrow
..... 2:30
GUNDAM ... 5:00
Cartoons
Discuss

WHAT THE H
CONVENTIO

SURE, HERE'S A PADDLE.

WET MOON

NOT **THAT** KIND OF PADDLE!

AW.

47

OKAY, GIRLS, HE CAN'T DANCE, BUT HE'S FLEXIBLE

HE CAN..... OH MY.

WOW!

I'M BIDDING FIVE BUCKS.

FAN FAN

THERE ARE BOYS WITH PRICE TAGS ALL AROUND ME!

GOOD GOD, I'VE GOT A HAREM.

I WAS SOLD TO JEN FOR $12.00

$1.50

ALRIGHT, BOYS,

NOW THAT I HAVE YOU...

...I GET TO DO WHATEVER I WANT WITH YOU.

WASH MY CAR.

50

PLAGUE MONKEY!

THE PLAGUE MONKEY ONLY KNOWS HOW TO DRAW WITH A SHARPIE.

FAMOUS LAST WORDS

ONE OUT OF **FOUR** AIN'T BAD.

SIGH.

I'M NEVER GOING TO GET PUBLISHED.

WHERE HAVE YOU APPLIED?

APPLY?

WHY ARE YOU EVEN TRYING? IT'S TOO HARD.

YOU'RE NOT GOING TO EXERCISE EVERY DAY, WHY BOTHER?

YOU'RE NOT GETTING ANY RESULTS. WHY ARE YOU EVEN TRYING?

PANT! PANT!

McDONALDS?

OOH YEAH!

IDEA™. OOH.

WHERE'S A PEN... GOTTA BE ONE SOMEWHERE ...COME ON!

I KNOW THERE'S ONE HERE...GOTTA FIND A PEN— DAMMIT–AH HAH!

CRAP.

FWUMP

FFAHAEA

THAT IS THE SOUND OF ULTIMATE SUFFERING!

I'M SO HAPPY.

THEY'RE JUST SO.... SO....

...THEY'RE THE MOST BEAUTIFUL THINGS I'VE EVER SEEN.

I LOVE MY MOMMY.

HAPPY B-DAY! LOVE: YO MAMMA

Batman Utility
belt ages 6-10
$12

DarthVader helmet
with voice adapter
$80

Flame Boots
from Mommy
$286

Best 25th
Birthday ever?
priceless

FAMOUS LAST WORDS

HAVE YOU GAINED WEIGHT?

I DON'T SEE HOW YOU CAN LIKE THOSE RAIL THIN WOMEN, THEY'VE GOT NO TITS OR ASS AND...

YOU NEED A BUCKET FOR THAT DROOL?

HELLO!

THE DEVIL'S PLAYTHING

DO YOU HAVE A NET?

WE GOT MEAT AS A BABY...

FROM A FRIEND WHOSE SNAKE WAS SICK...

SO MEAT WAS SUPPOSED TO BE....?

DINNER.

THANK YOU SO MUCH FOR LETTING US STAY WITH YOU DURING THE CONVENTION.

AND YOUR 14 CATS... AND 3 FERRETS... AND HORNY TOAD...

AND MEAT.

YEAH, UM BUN BYE.

SO HOW WAS THE CON?

I LOVE OUR LI'L EUNUCH.

SHE SMELLS FUNNY.

HOLY CRAP! WILL! THEY'RE GROWING!

I PLANTED DAFFODIL BULBS, AND I'VE NEVER GOTTEN ANYTHING TO **GROW** BEFORE.

TO COAX SOMETHING INTO THE **WARMTH AND LIGHT** OF **LIFE**.

IS THAT **SNOW?** GO BACK TO SLEEP!

FORTY-TWO.

BUT WHAT'S THE QUESTION?

THERE'S MY BOY. HOW YA DOIN', APOLLO?

GETTIN' KINDA PUDGY, HUH?

I'M NOT PUDGY!

I'M ROBUST.

CLICKCLICK

WHAT ARE YOU DOING?

TRYING TO TURN IT OFF.

I MET PATRICIA BRIGGS AT CONBUST AND HER BOOK
"DRAGON BONES" MADE ME BAWL AND IT'S JUST THE ASSHOLE WHO DIES!

SO, HOW DO YOU LIKE MY NEW HAIRCUT?

I DIDN'T KNOW BLACK GIRLS COULD GET A BOB. THE SWEATER'S CUTE TOO.

YOU KNOW WE'RE GOING TO A **GOTH** CLUB, RIGHT?

SHUT UP, AND GET IN THE TRUCK, BITCH.

VALLEY GIRL.

I DON'T GET YOU.

IT'S SO WARM OUT.

WHY DO YOU EVEN BOTHER WEARING A TRENCH COAT?

SO I DON'T GET PICKED UP ON THE STREET AS A PROSTITUTE.

NEW BOOTS?

THE MOST TERRIFYING, FANTABULOUS WOMAN I EVER MET GAVE THEM TO ME,

THEY LOOK GOOD.

THANKS.

THEY HURT LIKE HELL.

FAMOUS LAST WORDS.

YOU NEVER KNOW. YOU MIGHT LIKE IT.

WHEN WAS YOUR LAST VISIT?

1998.

GRACIOUS! WHY HAVE YOU WAITED SO LONG?

UM...

FEAR?

WHAT NOT TO SAY IN THE BEDROOM.

WHAT DO YOU MEAN THE BATTERY'S DEAD?!

-GILMORE

IF YOU'D LOCKED YOUR CAR...

IF YOU'D PARKED CLOSER TO THE HOUSE...

IF YOU'D JUST WALKED OUTSIDE...

IF YOU'D GONE OUT TO DINNER...

IF IF IF IF IF IF IF IF IF IF IF IF IF IF IF IF

IF YOU'D SHUT UP, I COULD GET ON WITH MY LIFE!

EEK

WACK WACK WAC FUCK!

BUT YOU'RE MY INSURANCE COMPANY! ISN'T THIS WHY I PAY YOU EVERY MONTH?!

WELL IF MY CAR'S FOUND IN A SCRAP HEAP, WILL YOU HELP ME WITH REPAIRS?!

WHAT DID THE INSURANCE COMPANY SAY ABOUT YOUR STOLEN CAR?

THEY SAID "SUCKS TO BE ME."

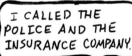

I CALLED THE POLICE AND THE INSURANCE COMPANY.

THERE'S NOTHING MORE THAT CAN BE DONE.

SNIFF. GOODBYE, HOOPTY.

HELLOOO, VESPA!

I SURVIVED THE DMV TO GET THE REPLACEMENT REGISTRATION...

...SO I COULD BAIL MY CAR OUT OF THE JUNKYARD, ONLY TO HAVE THE TOWTRUCK **NOT** SHOW UP FOR **THREE HOURS!**

NOW YOU GET YOUR TRUCK DRIVER'S **WIDE LOAD** ASS OUT HERE **NOW** OR I'LL HUNT YOU DOWN AND EAT YOUR **CHILDREN!!**

IS THIS WHAT THEY MEAN BY "BUILDING CHARACTER"?

CENSORED

SO THE CAR REPAIRS COST MORE THAN THE CAR IS WORTH, AND I GOTTA GET THE TITLE RE-ISSUED.

THE PLUMBER CHARGED ME $100 **NOT** TO FIX THE SINK, AND THE TOW COMPANY MESSED UP MY CREDIT INFO.

HI THERE, HOW ARE YOU DOING??

CENSORED

SEE BELOW*

*SOMETHING TO DO WITH THE UNIVERSE, A HOT IRON ROD COVERED WITH FIRE ANTS AND PENETRATION OF A VERY UNCOMFORTABLE PLACE,

I GOT CHINESE FOOD AND SOME DRAIN GEL FOR THE SINK.

HERE'S THE KEY TO MY OLD CAR, AND THERE'S A NEW "VENTURE BROTHERS" EPISODE TONIGHT.

OK, SO IT MIGHT HAVE TO DO WITH THE FACT THAT IT'S COLD IN THE NORTH AND HOT IN THE SOUTH, BUT I LIKE MY THEORY MORE.

84

85

SETH GREEN PLAYED DR. EVIL'S SON IN "AUSTIN POWERS"

WOULD YOU LIKE ME TO SIGN THIS?

MKAY.

PARDON ME, MR. GREEN, I'D LIKE YOU TO HAVE THIS.

OH, HEY DID YOU DRAW THIS?

YEAH, HOPE YOU LIKE IT.

THANKS!

THAT WAS VERY PROFESSIONAL OF YOU, JEN.

OHMYGOD OHMYGOD OHMYGOD OHMYGOD

SHE APPROACHED SETH GREEN IN A VERY PROFESSIONAL MANNER.

I ESPECIALLY LIKED THE PART WHERE SHE TRAMPLED THREE FIVE YEAR OLDS TO GET TO HIM.

BE AFRAID

I MET SETH GREEN I MET SETH GREEN I MET SETH GREEN I MET SETH GREEN I MET SETH GREEN I MET SETH GREEN I MET SETH GREEN I MET SETH GREEN

YOU DO REALIZE HE'S STILL BEHIND US, RIGHT?

YUP!

IT'S AN ONLINE AUTOBIOG—

I HAVE A **BANANA** IN MY POCKET!

oo

THE DEVIL'S PANTIES

...AT LEAST I **THINK** IT'S A BANANA...

YAY! MY SISTERS MADE IT TO THE CONVENTION!

THE DEVIL'S PANTIES.

SISTERS, THIS IS THE PIRATE AN HIS HORNY ELF FRIEND...

OKAY THANKS FOR VISITING, YOU SHOULD GO NOW... **RUN!**

THESE ARE MY SISTERS.

o0O0oh!

COMIXS

MY **BABY** SISTERS...

OH.

DON'T MISTAKE MY CONFIDENCE FOR COMPETENCE.

-CHRIS

PIRATE SAYS...

NIPPLES AREN'T FONDLING!

TEE HEE!

DJ, WHY DO YOU ALWAYS HAVE YOUR GUN WITH YOU?

BECAUSE THE SHOT GUN WOULD BE OVERKILL?

HEY, JEN, READY TO GET A PEDICURE?

YEAH, ONE MORE MINUTE.

WHAT ARE YOU DOING IN THERE?

SHAVING MY TOES.

THEY HAVE THE BEST CHAIRS FOR YOUR PEDICURE.

PRESS THAT BUTTON.

OH!..... OH MY.

WRRRR

THIS CHAIR HAS TOUCHED ME IN WAYS I'VE NEVER BEEN TOUCHED BEFORE.

HEY, I'LL BE DOING YOUR PEDICURE, YOU WANT A FOOT MASAGE?

UM...NO, THAT'S OKAY... THANKS.

LIFE'S "TO DO" LIST.

☑ Dance on a bar
☑ Go Go Boots
☑ Publish Comic
☑ Quit Day Job
☑ Get Flying MONKEY
☑ Cabana BOY
☐ Go To England
☐ MOVE to COUNTRY
☐ WO____tion
☐ Ch____

♪

BEING A GROWN UP MEANS...

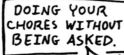

CALLING YOUR MOMMY ONLY AFTER YOU'VE FIXED IT.

DOING YOUR CHORES WITHOUT BEING ASKED.

GETTING WHAT YOU NEED BEFORE WHAT YOU WANT.

ICECREAM FOR DINNER.

WHAT NEVER TO SAY IN THE BEDROOM

IS IT SUPPOSED TO TASTE LIKE THAT?

HEY, JEN, I GOTTA PICK SOMETHING UP AT TARGÉ. WANNA COME?

SURE, JUST A SEC.

`KAY, I'M READY.

FAMOUS LAST WORDS

YOU READY FOR THE PARTY?

LEMME GET MY SHOES.

YOU'RE NOT GOING TO WEAR THAT **HAT** ARE YOU?

YOU'RE NOT ALLOWED TO CRITICIZE **MY** FASHION SENSE.

WHAT? IT'S AN **80's** PROM PARTY!

SO WHAT'S WITH THE TIN PLATES ON THE PEAR TREE?

JEN PUT THOSE UP TO SCARE THE SQUIRRELS OFF SO THE PEARS CAN RIPEN.

...SO HOW'S THAT WORKING FOR HER?

GRUMBLE.

FAMOUS LAST WORDS

BUT THIS'LL BE **FUN**.

DID THE NEW TREADMILL COME TODAY?

YEP, IT'S IN THE GARAGE.

YOU HAVEN'T TAKEN IT OUT OF THE BOX?

IT'S 200 LBS! **YOU** TAKE IT OUT OF THE BOX.

YOU KNOW YOU'RE A COUPLE WHEN...

CONNECT ROD **C** TO SPROCKET **XII**

FUG~~A~~ IT! **ROD** GOES IN THE **HOLE!** *CRUNCH* OR NOT.

NORDICKTRACK TREADMILL

PIRATE NINJA MONKEY

WHATCHA DOIN'?

BROWSING THE NET.

ARE YOU SHOPPING FOR **CELL PHONES** ON YOUR PHONE?!!

NO.

I'M SHOPPING FOR CELL PHONE **ACCESSORIES.**

ARE YOU **JUST** GETTING UP? OR... YOU'RE **STILL** UP, AREN'T YOU?

I FEEL FUNKY.

YOU FORGOT TO SLEEP AND EAT AGAIN.

OH!

STUPID ADDICTIONS.

SSHK

WAXING IS OVERRATED.

ZZZ

I'M SORRY, SIR, WE DON'T HAVE THAT ITEM IN STOCK.

NO SIR, THEY STOPPED PRINTING THAT ABOUT 20 YEARS AGO.

NO SIR, I WON'T CHECK E-BAY FOR YOU.

HAND ME CHOCOLATE OR A RIFLE, I DON'T CARE WHICH.

HEY, JEN, GOT A NEW WORKER.

THIS IS BETTY.

HI!

ESTROGEN!

I MEAN, HI.

SO THIS IS A STRESSFUL JOB?

NOT REALLY, YOU JUST— AH SHIT.

HEY SWEET CHEEKS, YOU EATIN' THAT CHOCOLATE HUH?

DON'TCHA KNOW IT'LL RUIN THAT CUTE GIRLISH FIGURE?

IT'S THE ONLY THING THAT'S KEEPING YOU ALIVE, MR. GOBS.

YOU JUST HAVE TO HAVE A HIGH TOLERANCE TO TESTOSTERONE.

SO WHAT'S A NICE GIRL LIKE YOU DO WHEN YOU'RE NOT WAITING ON GUYS LIKE ME?

WELL, I PLAY TROMBONE IN A BAND.

HEH HEH, I GOTTA TROMBONE YOU CAN PLAY.

GEE WHIZ SIR, I DON'T KNOW IF I SHOULD OVER-CHARGE YOU OR KICK YOU IN THE MOUTH.

HEY, ARIE, YOU ON YOUR WAY TO CHICAGO CON?

THE MANIACAL GIGGLING DOESN'T HELP, SWEETIE.

OR THE HYPERVENTILATING.

WHERE ARE YOU IN ILLINOIS?!

YAY! ARIE'S HERE!

LEMME GET MY OVERNIGHT STUFF...

WHERE DID I PUT THAT DUFFLE BAG?

EEK!

IS THAT *ARMOR?*

JUST IN CASE.

OH GOD, I GOT *SO* LOST.

I'VE GOT THE NAVIGATIONAL SENSE OF A STONED SQUIRREL.

SORRY, I'M TRYING TO PICTURE THAT.

Panel 1: OH, **WOW**, I SOLD OUT OF MY FLYERS!

Panel 2: LOOKS LIKE WE'RE DOING A MIDNIGHT PRINT RUN.

CLOSED

Panel 3: SO HOW LONG DO YOU THINK THIS WILL TAKE?

Panel 4: WHY DO YOU HAVE A **SLEEPING** BAG?

24 HOUR PRINTI

BAN $50

Panel 5: IT'S BEEN **HOURS** AND ALL THE PRINTS ARE **RUINED!**

Panel 6: THEY'RE NOT **CENTERED** AND THE FIRST 4 WORDS ARE **CUT OFF!**

COLOR COPIES

Panel 7: WELCOME TO **INDIE COMICS**, FUCK IT AND **CUT IT**.

Panel 8: IT'S SO **CUTE** WHEN YOU **WHIMPER**.

Panel 9: **FINALLY** DONE! **OOH**, THERE'S A TOY STORE.

LT TOYS   PRINTS

Panel 10: UH... WHAT KINDA TOY STORE IS OPEN AT THIS TIME OF NIGHT?

OPEN

Panel 11: **CUYOOT** LADYBUG TOYS!

Panel 12: JEN..... I DON'T THINK THAT'S WHAT YOU THINK IT IS...

IT'S SPARKLY!

BUT WHY DOES THIS PINK SPARKLY BUTTERFLY HAVE BATTERIES AND A HARNESS?

CLICK.

WRRR!

HOLY JUMPY SCROLL BUTTON.

ARE YOU LADIES FINDING EVERYTHING ALRIGHT?

UM.

WOULD YOU LIKE TO TEST IT BEFORE BUYING?

....DON'T TEASE.

I REALLY WANT TO BUY A BUTTERFLY.

HOW MUCH IS IT?

50$

BUY MY COMICS SO I CAN GET A TOY!

THE DEVIL'S PANTIES

106

MMM, CHECK OUT **HIS** ASS.

THE DEVIL'S PANTIES

JAILBAIT.

STAMINA.

I AM **NOT** A STARTER KIT.

THE DEVIL'S PANTIES

DO YOU HAVE THE CON PROGRAM? I WANNA FIND DAVID MACK.

SURE, HE'S RIGHT NEXT TO —

OHMYGOD- HOLYCRAP!

WOOSH!

WHO'S CARLA SPEED MCNEIL?

www.lightspeedpress.com

YOUR COMIC IS A PINPRICK VIEW INTO A BOUNDLESS WORLD.

YOUR INDEPENDENCE GIVES ME COURAGE TO FOLLOW MY OWN DREAM.

YOU'RE MY **ROLE MODEL**, MY **IDOL** MY **HERO!**

YOU'RE DROOLING ON MY ORIGINALS.

I'M REALLY GLAD YOU LIKE FINDER.

YOU KNOW, THE GUY NEXT TO ME LEFT IF YOU WANNA SET UP AT THE TABLE.

BREATHE IN...

FINDER- WWW.LIGHTSPEEDPRESS.COM

THANK YOU FOR LETTING ME GO TO DINNER AND ICE CREAM WITH YOU.

IT WAS FANTASTIC HANGING OUT WITH YOU.

NICE MEETING YOU.

GOOD BYE.

CRAP! I FORGOT TO ASK HER ABOUT COMIC PUBLISHING.

HEY, GUYS, I NEED YOU TO WRITE ME RENT CHECKS.

HERE YA GO.

THANKS.

PAYMENT FOR....

WAIT, WHAT'S "DONKEY PUNCH?"

CLICKETTY **CLICKCLICK** CLICKETTY CLICK CLICKCLICKCLICK CLICKETTY CLICK CLICK

DAMMIT, JEN, YOU'RE NOT USING ANY SKILL OR TECHNIQUE!

YOU'RE JUST PRESSING RANDOM BUTTONS!

AND I'M KICKING YOUR BUTT.

AND YOU'RE KICKING MY BUTT

GAME OVER

CONVENTION CENTER

DRAGON CON

I'M HOME!

ARE YOU JEN BREEDEN?

YEAH, I JUST GOT HERE. IT'S GOOD TO MEET YOU.

DO YOU NEED A HAND TO YOUR TABLE?

THANKS, BUT THIS IS MY "TABLE"

SIGH.

AND ME WITHOUT MY **LEAF BLOWER.**

DAMN! THEY'RE OUT OF **PARFAIT**

I **HATE** IT THAT THEY'RE ALWAYS OUT BEFORE I GET UP TO THE FRONT.

MAYBE IF WE ASK POLITELY...

WE REQUIRE **PARFAIT.**

THIS IS **SO MUCH** FUN!

I FEEL FUNNY.

HAVE YOU EATEN?

SURE! I HAD A **BAGLE** THIS MORNING!

HON, IT'S 8:00 PM.

YEP. THAT WOULD DO IT.

"BUBBA" THE REDNECK WEREWOLF BY MITCH HYMAN

"BUBBA" THE REDNECK WEREWOLF BY MITCH HYMAN

"BUBBA" THE REDNECK WEREWOLF BY MITCH HYMAN

"BUBBA" THE REDNECK WEREWOLF BY MITCH HYMAN

WHY DON'T YOU GO JUMP HIM?

NO...NO, I'M TAKEN. BESIDES, I NEVER TRY ANYTHING ON...

...I JUST **WINDOW** SHOP.

DO YOU NEED A HAND TO YOUR ROOM?

SURE.

INCOMING!

CLICK

OH! I'M SORRY!

DIAMOND

DON'T BE, IT'S NAKED TIME!

I LOVE DRAGONCON.

JOY! AT LEAST **SOME** OF THE PIRATES ARE HERE!

HEY, HON.

UH, WHAT'S WITH SPIDER GUY?

DON'T TALK TO HIM, HE'S A PERV.

WOOHOO!

IT'S HIS FIRST TIME AT DRAGON CON.

AH.

WE GOT SPIDER GUY TO POSE FOR US BACK AT THE HOTEL.

OH MY GOD, THAT'S JUST **WRONG!**

SPIDER GUY, HOW **COULD** YOU!?

EASY, I JUST USED CLAMPS AND A **LOT** OF LUBE.

I.D. OR SCREENING.

I FORGOT MY I.D. SO I GUESS I'LL HAVE A SCREENING.

YOU'RE 25. **HOLY CRAP,** YOU'RE **GOOD!**

THAT'S WHAT HAPPENS WHEN YOU'RE A BOUNCER FOR 15 YEARS.

WEE HEE! HOOOOO!

WHAT DID YOU **GIVE** HER?!

PIXY STIX AND KOOL-AID.

HOUSTON, WE HAVE LIFTOFF.

SAY **HI** ATLANTA!!

DAMN, THEY'RE OUT OF BOOZE.

SAYS *YOU*...

SWIG.

DAMN, IT'S GOOD TO BE A CHEAP DRUNK!

HERE, HAVE A SCOTCH.

THANKS.

LET ME JUST GET THIS MASK OFF...

SPIDER GUY IS *HOT!*

AND A PERV.

DAMN, BUT I LOVE A DRUM CIRCLE!

WHAT **NEVER** TO SAY IN THE BEDROOM.

WHAT'S FOREPLAY?

GIRL COP PEZ DISPENSER

YOUR BOOBS GOT SMALL.

GIRL RULE

OOH! OOH!

DO MINE! DO MINE!

BREST INSPECTOR

WHY ARE THE BOOBS GONE?!

HON, I DROPPED 50 POUNDS AND I BENCHPRESS 130 POUNDS.

I FUCKED YOUR GIRLFRIEN

KED RIEND

BUT WHY ARE THE BOOBS GONE?!

HEY, DJ?

HM?

IS THIS A PART FROM YOUR PEZ DISPENSER...

OR YOUR STRAP-ON?

HMM...

I LOVE US.

SO THEN I WAS DRUNK...

...AND WHEN I'M **DRUNK**, THEN I GET **HORNY**...

...AND WHEN I'M **HORNY**, THEN I WANT TO **FIGHT**...

AND I THOUGHT **MY** JOB WAS HARD!

YOU HAVE **NO** IDEA.

HEY, JEN, WHAT'S THAT IN YOUR BACK POCKET?

HUH?

IT'S MY **ASS!**

OH.

HEY, AILI...

WHAT'S THIS SPIDERWEB WALL CHART?

DJ TRIED TO TRACK HER LOVE LIFE.

FAMOUS LAST WORDS/WHAT **NEVER** TO SAY IN THE BEDROOM.

SO....WHAT ARE THE PADDLES FOR?

OOOH...TOO MUCH ICE-CREAM.

I'M **COLD** ON THE **INSIDE.**

QUICK, SOMEONE GET SOMETHING **WARM IN HER!**

UM.

READY TO GO CLUBBING?

ALMOST!

GOOD **LORD**, WOMAN!

LET'S PLAY "SPOT THE SOUTHERNER."

IT'S **COLD!**

DID YOU SEE HER **SKIRT?**

NO.

NEITHER DID I.

HEY SWEETIE! **LAUREN!**

I GOT YOU A PRESENT.

AW, IT'S A CUTE LITTLE—

OH! MY GOD!

WRRRRRRr

SO DID YOU TRY IT OUT?

YOU MUST BE MY **FAIRY GOD**MOTHER!

SSHH.

OOPS.

WHAT NEVER TO SAY IN THE BEDROOM.

FOR MICHELLE, THE ULTIMATE BROAD

WHAT NEVER TO SAY IN THE BEDROOM.

UH.... **WHAT?!**

GOOD **GOD**, THAT'S A BEAUTIFUL PERSON.

I THINK THAT'S A BOY.

BONUS.

YOU KNOW, WE COULD INTRODUCE YOU.

WHAT?! AND RUIN THE STALKER FUN?!

LOVE YOU GUYS, BUT IT'S FRIGGIN' **COLD** UP HERE!

WHEN ARE WE GOING TO MEET THE NONEXISTENT BOY OF YOURS?

WHEN YOU COME DOWN SOUTH TO VISIT ME.

ARE YOU **KIDDING?!** IT'S **SWELTERING** DOWN THERE!

WHAT NEVER TO SAY IN THE BEDROOM.

IS THAT **WITH** TAX?

AH HA! I FOUND MY WALLET!

NOW I DON'T HAVE TO DO MY **LAUNDRY** TO FIND IT.

YOUR LOGIC IS IMPECCABLE.

SHREEK!

GIGGLE!

CHASE ME **NOW**, BITCHES.

NGH!

WAAA!

WAAA!

WAAA!

I WANTED TO GET **HAMSTERS**.

HEY, HON, COULD YOU GET ME A GLASS OF MILK?

NO.

HA HA! MY GIRLFRIEND WOULD GET ME MILK IF I ASKED HER TO...

...BUT I **LOVE** AND **RESPECT** HER TOO MUCH TO DEGRADE HER IN SUCH A FASHION....

GOOD BOY.

WHAT NEVER TO SAY IN THE BEDROOM.

HOW OWNING A DOG PREPARES A MAN FOR DATING A WOMAN.

HOW OWNING A DOG
PREPARES A MAN FOR
DATING A WOMAN.

WHAT NOT TO SAY IN THE BEDROOM.

WHO'S CAROL?!

BY TERRY

PEOPLE SEEM INTELLIGENT ENOUGH...

...BUT THEN WHEN IT COMES DOWN TO VOTING ON SOMETHING, EVERYTHING GOES TO HELL!

YEEEAH.

AW, WILL, YOUR PANTS ARE FALLING DOWN.

YANK!

I'M HELPING!

FIRST DAY OF CAR HUNTING...

NO, I DON'T LIKE THE TINTED WINDOWS.

24TH DAY OF CAR HUNTING...

FUCK IT, GIVE ME ANYTHING, JUST LET IT HAVE WHEELS!

FLIP!

FLIP!

YOU KNOW THERE'S A CAR THAT GOES WITH THAT.

BUT THIS KEY IS SO COOL!

WHAT'S A NIPPLE CLAMP?

WHAT NOT TO SAY IN THE BEDROOM.

BY JIM

145

HI, JEN.

UH, HEY.

WHO WAS THAT?

MOLLY.

YOU MEAN LITTLE MOLLY WITH THE **HUGE** GLASSES WHO I USED TO **BABYSIT** FOR, MOLLY?

YUP.

BUT THEY'RE NOT **SUPPOSED** TO GROW UP **BEFORE** ME!!

WHAT? I'M **JEWISH!**

I'M GONNA GET IN **SO** MUCH TROUBLE FOR THIS.

BREEDEN FAMILY TRADITION...

EMBARRASS MOM AT THE X-MAS EVE SERVICE.

MAKE SOMEONE CRY ON CHRISTMAS DAY.

WAIT AT THE TOP OF THE STAIRS ON X-MAS MORNING AND STAMPEDE DOWN.

ANATOMICALLY CORRECT X-MAS COOKIES.

HERE, JEN, MERRY X-MAS.

CLANG!

I MADE YOU A **SHIELD** FOR WHEN YOU RUN AROUND IN THE WOODS AND HIT PEOPLE WITH PADDED STICKS.

PADDED IS THE OPERATIVE WORD HERE.

SO HOW'S LITTLE PRINCESS PORCELAIN?

FOOD?

WELL, SHE'S ALRIGHT...

FOOD!

BUT AFTER SHE STARTED PEEING OUT OF HER NAVEL...

FOOD! FOOD!

YOU REALIZED HE WAS A **PRINCE** PORCELAIN?

YUP.

FOOD! YOU WILL BE.

SO YOUR PIG'S A BOY. YOU GOING TO CHANGE HIS NAME?

WELL WE WERE THINKING ABOUT NAMING HIM—

CRASH!

LITTLE **FUCKER!** GET OUT OF THERE!

HOW'S THE COMIC BOOK COMING?

WHAT NOT TO SAY IN THE BEDROOM.

SO..... THAT'S IT?

BY TERRY

AAH WINTER.

NOTHING LIKE A CUP OF HOT COCOA AND A BIG BLANKET!

OKAY, IT'S FUCKIN' COLD! WHEN'S SUMMER GOING TO GET HERE!?

HELLO, COMIC SHOP- OH, SORRY SIR. THE BIBLE BINDER MOVED.

OH, ALRIGHT, WELL REMEMBER THAT JESUS LOVES YOU.

UH... OKAY. BYE.

CLICK.

NO I DON'T.

I KNOW.

ANSWERS TO "JESUS LOVES YOU"

YEAH? WELL THE GODDESS COULD GIVE A SHIT ABOUT YOU!

AND BUDDHA LOVES YOU, SIR!

NO HE DOESN'T. HE SAID SO.

BUT WE'RE JUST FRIENDS.

HACHEE MOMMA!!

HOT GUYS IN COMICS ARE FEW AND FAR IN BETWEEN.

SO, THEY MUST BE CELEBRATED AT EVERY OPPORTUNITY WHEN FOUND.

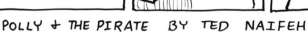

POLLY & THE PIRATE   BY TED NAIFEH

YAY! WHAT THE HELL CON!

GOTTA LOVE COLLEGE CONVENTIONS. LOW STRESS, FUN, PERSONABLE...

 GINGERBREAD SPOOGE!

OPENING CEREMONIES WTHC

 ..."SPECIAL" DOESN'T COVER IT.

WHAT NOT TO SAY IN THE BEDROOM

HONEY, DO YOU HAVE A VACUUM CLEANER?

GEEK...

SCARY GEEK...

GEEK...

SCARY GEEK...

PATRICK STEWART IS **GOD**.

BEAM ME UP

IF PATRICK STEWART TOLD ME TO, I'D KILL ANYONE IN THIS ROOM.

TRUE BELIEVER

OH **WOW!** MY FAVORITE CARTOONIST! I LOVE YOU!

DING DONG!

WHAT ARE YOU MAKING?

A TRIBUTE TO MY HOMELAND.

....DUDE, YOU'RE FROM CANADA.

HUSH!

ARE YOU GOING FOR EXTRA BROWNIE POINTS?

I GOT THROWN OUT OF GIRL SCOUTS...

...FUCK BROWNIE POINTS.

YOU READY FOR THE GEEK AUCTION?

YUP!

RESERVED FOR JEN'S HAREM

OH, THIS IS GOING TO BE FUN!

NOW LADIES, AS TO THE FOUL LANGUAGE, SEXUAL INNUENDOS, AND ADULT CONTENT...

...WE TRY TO ENCOURAGE THAT, ALONG WITH ABJECT HUMILIATION.

REMIND ME **WHY** WE'RE DOING THIS.

RAVENOUS GIRLS SCREAMING FOR YOUR BODY?

OH YEAH.

ALRIGHT, LADIES, WELCOME TO THE **GEEK** AUCTION!

WOHOO!

I'M SCARED.

YOU **SHOULD** BE.

I WILL **PAY** YOU TO PUT YOUR SHIRT **BACK** ON.

WHO WANTS TO **FEED** MY **MONKEY?**

HEAR THAT? THAT'S THE SOUND OF DROOLING.

BUY IN **BULK!**

AND WHAT'S YOUR ALIGNMENT?

AWFUL GOOD— I MEAN LAWFUL! LAWFUL GOOD.

SHE MEANT SEXUAL ALIGNMENT.

I LIKE THE GIRLS?

MM HMM.

SO, ARE YOU GOING TO WHIP IT OUT?

UM...

SHE MEANT YOUR WHIP SILLY BOY!

OH! WELL I DON'T KNOW IF THERE'S ENOUGH ROOM FOR ME TO TAKE IT OUT.

YOU KNOW, I DON'T THINK INDIANA JONES HAD A SHIRT ON UNDER HIS LEATHER COAT.

OH, OKAY.

I BID $5.

FOOMP!

 YANK!

 ...AND JEN BIDS 20$! 69

 OH, THAT'S JUST **WRONG!**

 YET, **SO** MANY KINDS OF **RIGHT!**

 HEY, JEN, YOU BID ON INDIANA JONES? YEAH.

 EVERYTHING I HAVE IS YOURS.

 OH.... I'M IN A **SPECIAL** PLACE.

WHAT NEVER TO SAY IN THE BEDROOM...

RING

HELLO?

HEY, JEN, THE BROAD'S IN TOWN...

...WANNA DO FONDUE?

FONDUE?

3 SIGNS OF A REAL WOMAN, BY THE BROAD™

Ms. BROAD
#1.
#2.
#3.

WHACK!

#1. SHE BITCH SLAPS HER MAN...

YES, DEAR?

#2. SHE ROLLS HER OWN TAMPONS...

#3. SHE KICK STARTS HER VIBRATOR.

HUNNUN NUN UN UN

OH, AND WE GOT PILLOWS TODAY.

PILLOWS?

FOR OUR BRAS!

GOOO GOD WOMAN, THEY'RE GINORMOUS!!

YEAH.

166

TABLE FOR FOUR?

OH, WOW, I NEED TO BUY YOU A DRINK.

WILL YOU TAKE MY NUMBER?

THE PILLOWS ARE GOOD.

You had to be there...

SHE CAN SIT ON ICE CREAM AND TELL YOU WHAT FLAVOR IT IS.

HE NEEDS STRIPES TO TELL IF HE'S ROLLIN' OR STROLLIN'.

DAME VS. BROAD.

A DAME IS A GIRLY GIRL...

...A **BROAD** CAN **LOOK** LIKE A DAME....

...BUT SHE CAN CHANGE HER OWN TIRE...

...ON HER WAY TO THE COCKTAIL PARTY.

GOOD EVENING LADIES...

...WOULD YOU LIKE TO BEGIN WITH A SALAD?

LITTLE BOY, BRING US A COW AND BACK AWAY!

MY NUMBER IS 555-6239.

YOU WANNA HAVE FUN?

HOW MUCH FUN?

I BROUGHT BAIL MONEY.

HEY, HON, CAN I TOUCH YOU INAPPROPRIATELY?

WE'VE FORGOTTEN ALL ABOUT OUR TOKEN MALE.

OH, HE LOVES HAVING BEAUTIFUL WOMEN ALL UP ON HIM.

YEAH, THE OPERATIVE WORD BEING **BEAUTIFUL**.

IF WE'RE GONNA TRASH TALK, THEN I'LL NEED ANOTHER DOUBLE.

THE BROAD

DON'T YOU MISS ME, BABY?

YEAH...

...BUT I'VE BEEN WORKING ON MY AIM.

WHAT HE SAID.

WHAT HE MEANT.

WHAT SHE HEARD.

WHAT SHE SAID...

I WOULDN'T EVEN SLEEP WITH YOU IF I WAS DRUNK.

I WOULDN'T TAKE ADVANTAGE OF YOU BECAUSE I RESPECT YOU AND VALUE OUR RELATIONSHIP.

I WOULDN'T TOUCH YOU WITH A TEN FOOT POLE, **SKANK!**

WELL, OFFICER, WHAT HAPPENED WAS...

THE BROAD

I DIDN'T ESCAPE, THEY GAVE ME A **DAY** PASS!

MA'AM, WOULD YOU PLEASE HOLD?

SURE...

...AS LONG AS YOU KNOW THAT I'M DOING A TEQUILA SHOT FOR EVERY MINUTE I'M ON HOLD.

UH OH.

CAN'T SLEEP...

...CABLE GUY MIGHT CALL...

RING

HELLO!?

THIS IS THE CABLE COMPANY. HOW WAS THE SERVICE YOU RECEIVED?

WHAT SERVICE!?

FUCKING CABLE BULL... I'LL TEAR... RIP... INTE... AND PUT... SEV... ELLS AND GR... AT MY FEE... THE DEV... THE GO... OUT EY... HE... ON EARTH.

WHAM! CRASH! WHUMP CRINKLE

I FOUND MY CHOCOLATE STASH...

...THE UNIVERSE MAY LIVE.

I'M REALITY CHALLENGED.

SO, YOUR BOOK'S PUBLISHED?

UNATTENDED CHILDREN WILL BE SOLD

YUP! LIFE'S GOAL ACHIEVED AT THE AGE OF TWENTY-SIX.

THAT WAS YOUR LIFE'S GOAL?

I OWN A HOUSE, SUPPORT MYSELF, AND MY ART'S GOING ACROSS THE WORLD. WHAT MORE IS THERE?

SPAY YOUR CAT-GIRL

MOST WOMEN'S LIFE GOAL IS TO GET MARRIED AND HAVE KIDS.

BWAHAHAHAHA!

YOU'RE FUNNY.

HEY JEN, WE FOUND **PORN!**

FOUND PORN? BUT IT'S A TOY SNAKE.

RAPID TONGUE ACTION!

WRRR

HEY, JEN, WE GOT BURRITOS, WANT ONE?

WHOOMP!

A SIMPLE "YES" WOULD HAVE BEEN FINE.

THAT'S MY **HAND!** QUIT GNAWING!

MUNCH MUNCH

MUNCH MUNCH

LOOK, IT'S **FUZZY!** HAVE SOME.

I'M NOT PUTTING THAT IN MY MOUTH.

THAT'S THE FIRST TIME YOU'VE EVER SAID **THAT.**

I couldn't decide which cartoon aptly described my delight and the other bathroom attendants bewilderment.

BY JIM

182

FANTSY PANTS SUPER STARS

ARTIST'S ALLEY

WHY DO I KNOW THAT CACTUS?

GASP! GIRLS WITH SLINGSHOTS!

SCREE

CHEESE!

OOH, THIS IS THE CUTEST PICTURE EVER!

GWS

I AM SO MASTURBATING TO THIS LATER.

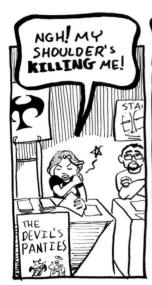

NGH! MY SHOULDER'S **KILLING** ME!

THE DEVIL'S PANTIES

YOU WANT ME TO WORK ON IT?

SURE!

NOW RELAX...

I CAN'T!

REMEMBER, IT'LL HURT LESS IF YOU DON'T RESIST...

HOW ARE WE GONNA FIND YOUR SISTER?

JAIL BAIT

EEK!

MWHAHAH!

JUST FOLLOW THE SCREAMS.

JAIL BAIT

SO, BIG SIS...

THE DEVIL'S PANTIES

...I'LL BE GRADUATING FROM COLLEGE NEXT WEEK...

...NOW COULD YOU **PLEASE** STOP WITH THE **JAIL BAIT**?

NEVER!

JAIL BAIT

HEY, JEN...

...I BIT THE INSIDE OF MY LIP.

SHEE?

YOU'RE SO PRETTY.

HI, I'M...

...MIKE.

WHY DID YOU HAVE TO LOOK AT MY CHEST TO REMEMBER YOUR **NAME**?

OH MY.

WELL THAT HAS GOT TO BE THE **FINEST** ASS I'VE SEEN IN SPANDEX.

THE DEVIL'S PANTIES

HEY SPIDEY, I LIKE YOUR BUTT!

YOU HAVE NO SHAME.

WHAT'S SHAME?

JOSHUA SMITH

IT WAS GOOD SEEING YOU, LITTLE SIS. WHAT ARE YOU GONNA DO NOW THAT YOU GRADUATED?

I'M GOING TO NEW ZEALAND, FIJI, AND AUSTRALIA.

EVERYTHING'S POISONOUS IN AUSTRALIA AND BOYS HAVE COOTIES!!

MMMM... COOTIES.

WHIMPER.

HEY, WILL, I'M HOME.

COOL, DID YOU GET THE CAT A NEW FUZZY TOY?

PLEASE SAY YES!

HEY, YOUR SISTER WANTS ME TO PAINT A MURAL IN HER NURSERY.

I'M DRIVING TO SAVANNAH FOR THE BABY SHOWER...

SO...DO I HAVE TO GO TOO?

YES!

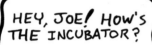

HEY, JOE! HOW'S THE INCUBATOR?

SHE'S ON THE COUCH.

HEY, BRO, WANNA SAY "HI" TO THE TWINS?

AAAH!

I AM UNAMUSED.

WHAT NEVER TO SAY IN THE BEDROOM.

AW, **DEER!**

OOH, DEER!

MMM, DEER.

WHEEZE HACK

WHOSE IDEA WAS THIS?!

PUFF

I'M GONNA DIE.

I HATE YOU.

PUFF

SAME TIME NEXT WEEK?

YEAH.

GRUMBLE MUMBLE...

...I HAD TO DO THIS ONCE ALREADY IN LIFE...

...IT'S MY REALITY, AND I'LL HAVE FLYING MONKEYS IF I WANT TO.

I WANT MY FLYING MONKEYS!

FAIRY GODMOTHER!

HEY, HON, WELCOME TO PHILLY.

THIS IS OUR INTERN. BE NICE!

DON'T WORRY, I ONLY BITE THOSE I LOVE.

I LIKE HER!!

HEY, GRAN'MA, THANKS FOR GIVING US A RIDE TO THE CONVENTION.

NO PROBLEM, SWEETIE.

YOU KNOW, IF I COULD STILL GET SOME, I WOULD.

OHMYGOD! JEN FROM "DEVIL'S PANTIES"!

HOLYCRAP, IT'S CIQUE FROM "IN THE PUDDLE"!

I'M YOUR BIGGEST FAN!!

THIS WOULD BE PATHETIC IF IT WASN'T SO ADORABLE.

WWW.INTHEPUDDLE.COM

197

WHAT NEVER TO SAY IN THE BEDROOM.

WHAT DO YOU **MEAN** IT'S BROKEN!?

SO HOW DO YOU PROMOTE YOUR COMIC AT CONVENTIONS?

THE DEVIL'S PANTIES

FOOMP.

TAKE MY CARD OR THE JLA VARIANT COVER GETS IT!

JLA

PIRATE! JEN!

GROPE

GROPE
GROPE
GRO
GROPE

HOW'RE THINGS?

YOU'VE BEEN WORKING OUT.

8 ♣

8 ♣

HEY! WHO ARE YOU FUCKING?

UMM... YOU?

WELL DONE.

YOU PEOPLE STILL THINK I'M MAKING THIS SHIT UP.

YOU WANNA GO TO A GOTH CLUB?

HMMM.

NO! YOU'RE TOO TIRED.

THE PLAGUE MONKEY WILL GET YOU!

GOTH CLUB!

HOW OFTEN DO YOU GET TO GO TO A GOTH CLUB IN NEW YORK FUCKING CITY!

OKAY!

WHERE'D SHE GO?

DAMN YOUR INDECISION.

WE BROUGHT YOU CODE RED MOUNTAIN DEW AND RED BULL.

DRINK HALF THE DEW AND ADD THE RED BULL!

ARE YOU TRYING TO **KILL** ME?!

NOT DIRECTLY.

WE WANNA SEE WHAT HAPPENS.

HI, ARE YOU AN **ARTIST**?

WANNA COME UP TO MY HOTEL ROOM AN' I'LL **REVIEW** YOUR **PORTFOLIO**?

WHACK!

YOU'RE INTERNING WITH **SILENT DEVIL**, AREN'T YOU?

IT'S NOT MY FAULT!

WHAT NEVER TO SAY IN THE BEDROOM.

SURVIVAL GUIDE FOR CONVENTIONS.

PUBLIC SERVICE ANNOUNCEMENT

"REVIEW YOUR PORTFOLIO" IS MAKING OUT...

...AND SHARPIE BODY ART IS FOREPLAY.

WHAT'S THAT ON YOUR ELBOW?

UM.

BAD BEARS DON'T HAVE MOUTHS!

THE DEVIL'S PANTIES

THEY MESS UP YOUR HARD DRIVE...

I THINK I JUST MET MYSELF FROM AN ALTERNATE REALITY.

WHACK!
WHACK!
WHACK!

HOW MANY OF THOSE "AIRBORN" VITAMINS HAVE YOU HAD??

THE PLAGUE MONKEY SHALL NOT WIN!!

THE DEVIL'S PANTIES

UPDO STUDI

HMM, WHERE'S THE MOST TENDER SPOT FOR ME TO WALK ACROSS.

HOLY CRAP!

DON'T LOOK! IT'S KEVIN SMITH.

BE VEWY VEWY QUIET, WE'RE HUNTING CEWEBWITIES.

EEASY...
...EASY...

...DON'T MAKE ANY SUDDEN MOVES....

DAMN, HE'S MAKING A RUN FOR IT!

I LOVE YOU KEVIN SMITH!

ONCE UPON A TIME...

WOULD YOU LIKE TO BE THE FIRST EVER TO BUY A DEVIL'S PANTIES COMIC BOOK?

I WOULD, BUT I SPENT ALL MY MONEY ON GRAVY BOY.

CURSE YOU GRAVY BOY.

CURSE YOU!

GRAVYBOY!

CRASH

JEN, I'M GONNA TAKE YOU TO MY ROLLER DERBY CLASS!

ISN'T ROLLER DERBY WHERE THE GIRLS TRY AND KILL EACH OTHER ON SKATES?

YUP.

THIS IS GONNA BE SO MUCH FUN!

EEK?

HEY, JEN, YOU READY FOR ROLLER DERBY CLASS?

JUST ABOUT.

I CAN BRAKE EVERY BONE IN MY BODY EXCEPT MY **DRAWING HAND!**

SIZE EIGHT ROLLER SKATES PLEASE!

HERE YA' GO. I'LL NEED TO HOLD ONTO YOUR SHOES.

MY.... MY **BABIES?**

BUT THEY'VE NEVER BEEN TO **DAY CARE** BEFORE!

WHAT NOT TO SAY IN THE BEDROOM.

THEY'RE **NOT** EDIBLE?!

HEY, HON, WHAT ARE YOU—

IS THAT A PRINTOUT OF THE USER'S MANUAL OF THAT CAR YOU WANT?

IT'S SOOO PRETTY.

OKAY, WILL, YOU'RE JUST TEST DRIVING THIS CAR. YOU CAN'T AFFORD TO BUY IT YET.

VROOM

WHO AM I KIDDING?

WHAT?!

KROOM
OH MY GOD!

VROOOOOM
OOOH WOW.

DAMNIT WILL!

THIS CAR IS GETTING YOU TO MAKE NOISES THAT I CAN'T EVEN GET YOU TO MAKE!

WANNA GO FOR A DRIVE?

SURE, LET ME GET MY STUFF.

WALLET, DAY PLANNER, PHONE, TAPE RECORDER FOR CARTOON IDEAS...

...CAMERA FOR REFERENCE SHOTS AND CAR KEYS.

READY!

I NEED A BAG FOR ALL THIS STUFF.

YOU MEAN A PURSE?

NO!

FACE IT, HON, YOU'RE TURNING INTO A GIRL.

TODAY IS THE DAY THAT I SHALL VANQUISH THE RED DOT OF DOOM!

I NEED A LAPTOP SO I CAN CHECK MAIL AT CONVENTIONS.

BUT I DON'T WANNA SPEND MORE THAN 300$.

YOU CAN GET A NEW CELL PHONE THAT HAS INTERNET FOR $300.

BUT I *LOVE* MY BRICK!

NO, I LOVE MY **BRICK**. IT HAS THREE BUTTONS AND I KNOW HOW TO USE THEM.

THIS HAS A CAMERA, NOTE PAD, RECORDER, DAY PLANNER, MUSIC, VIDEO, INTERNET, AND GPS.

YOU MEAN I WOULDN'T HAVE TO GET A PURSE?

I LOVE YOU GUYS, BUT THIS CAN'T GO ON!

YOU PUT YOUR SCHEDULE IN AND IT REMINDS YOU BEFORE YOU HAVE TO BE THERE.

BING AT 9:45PM KICK EVERYONE OUT OF THE COMIC SHOP FOR CLOSING TIME.

I HAVE MY FLYING MONKEY!

HI, I MADE YOU A BOOK AND ETCHED YOUR CHARACTERS ON THE FRONT.

OH, WOW!

SNFF!! LEATHER!

GOOD GOD WOMAN, THAT'S TREATED! THE FUMES WILL, WELL, WEE!

TAKE A CARD! PINK GOES WITH EVERYTHING!

HULLO,...OH. 'EY THINK 'AVE SEEN THIS.

IF 'EY BUY ONE, COULD YE' SIGN IT?

ONLY IF YOU KEEP TALKING!

IT'S TIME FOR THE WEBCOMIC ARTIST AUCTION.

EVERYONE'S HAD THEIR SHOTS, RIGHT?

I'VE HIDDEN A HAIRBALL SOMEWHERE IN THIS HOUSE.

NEXT UP FOR AUCTION IS THE CREATOR OF THE DEVIL'S PANTIES.

HEH. HEH. HEH.

BID AT YOUR OWN RISK.

SOLD! TO THE GENTLEMAN IN THE BACK.

HI!

YOU KNOW WE JUST HANG OUT, RIGHT?

I LIKE BACON.

YAY FOR BACON!

223

www.sluggy.com

HEY, WILL! I WENT TO THE FARMERS MARKET AND GOT ALL THIS COOL STUFF!

WHAT'S THIS?

SUGAR CANE!

HOW DO YOU EAT IT?

I HAVE NO IDEA.

HEY, HON?

HMM?

ON THE LIST OF CAR, CAT, GIRLFRIEND, WHERE EXACTLY DO I FALL?

UM...

RUN DUDE.

OH WOW! WAPSI SQUARE! I'VE GOT A TON OF QUESTIONS ABOUT CHARACTER DESIGN AND STORY PACING.

DON'T GEEK OUT! DON'T GEEK OUT!

GOOD YOU DRAW!

THANKS.

DAMMIT!

WHACK!

THE CONVENTION IS CLOSED FOR TODAY.

ONLY EXHIBITORS WITH BADGES ARE ALLOWED ON THE FLOOR.

FWIP

I NEED TO BE THROWN OUT!

— MARC

229

WOOO!

SORRY, THAT'S JUST MY CANE.

BUT YES, I **AM** HAPPY TO SEE YOU.

THAT'S THE NICEST THING THAT'S HAPPENED TO ME SINCE DARTH MAUL **GOOSED** ME.

WANT SOME COFFEE AND BAILEYS?

SURE!

OH MY! YOU KNOW, THIS IS SO HORRIBLE THAT I'M GOING TO HAVE TO SAVE YOU FROM IT BY DRINKING IT ALL MYSELF.

I APPRECIATE YOUR SACRIFICE AS A FRIEND AND A HUMAN BEING...

...BUT FUCK OFF.

WHAT NOT TO SAY IN THE BEDROOM.

I HAVE A CONFESSION TO MAKE...

CAN I GET MY PICTURE WITH YOU?

SURE!

IN THE PUDDLE!

BONGOS!

WE MADE YOU A FLYING MONKEY!

Oooo! SO SOFT!

TOUCH MY MONKEY!!

ARE YOU A PIRATE?

WHY **YES**, MILADY, THAT I AM!

MY MOMMY **WARNED** ME ABOUT MEN LIKE **YOU**.

GROAN, I COULD SLEEP FOR ANOTHER TWENTY MINUTES...

...OR I COULD GO BUY A LEAF BLOWER FOR DRAGON CONVENTION...

BREET! BREET! BREET!

BEEP.

HEY, LADY, WHAT'S WITH THE LEAFBLOWER?

I'M HUNTING **KILTS!**

EXCUSE ME, SIR, WOULD YOU LIKE TO BE IN A "MEN IN KILTS" CALENDAR?

SURE.

GIRLS, ARE YOU READY?

SIR, ARE YOU READY?

UH.

DON'T WORRY, SIR, I'M A PROFESSIONAL!

PROFESSIONAL **WHAT?**

HOW COULD YOU THINK THAT I'D BE **OKAY** WITH THAT?!?

WHICH WAY DID HE GO?

WHO?

WE'RE **FAIRY** HUNTING!

YOU KNOW, HIS GIRLFRIEND'S OVER THERE, YOU COULD GET HIS CELL # AND ASK WHERE HE IS.

BUT THAT'S NO **FUN.**

ONLY AT DRAGON CON...

DO YOU WANT MY PIXY STICK?

♪

HOLY **GODDESS!**

OH! YOU'RE JENNIE. I'M A BIG FAN.

YES. YES YOU ARE.

236

CAN I GET MY PICTURE WITH YOU?

YOU WANT A PICTURE WITH ME??

FLASH!

I KNITTED YOU A FLYING MONKEY HAT.

OH WOW!

COME BY MY BOOTH. I WANNA TIE YOU UP!

UM...?

IN A CORSET, SILLY.

RIGHT.

2
♠
♠

WHAT NOT TO SAY IN THE BEDROOM.

MISSED!!

-- Steve

READY?

UM...

ARMS UP, BREATH OUT, AND-

HURK!

HOW IS IT?

THE WORDS "STEEL DRUM" COMES TO MIND.

HI!

WHAT ARE YOU DOING TONIGHT?

BRUTE FORCE

ME.

BACK OFF, KITTEN, BEFORE I HAVE TO SCRAPE THOSE PIXIE WINGS OFF OF MY BOOT.

238

DAMMIT.

MY MONKEY'S FLAT.

COULD YOU BLOW IT UP FOR ME?

'KAY.

I COULD BE A MONKEY.

CAN I GET A PICTURE OF YOU LADIES?

SURE.

FLASH!

I THINK YOU'VE BEEN A BAD INFLUENCE ON ME.

WHO, ME?

It took twelve hours, but we finally made it into Dragon Con!

I suddenly want to burn something.

You're listening to the wrong conscience.

Nope, they're both saying that.

Have you slept at all this weekend?

Maaybe?

If you don't sleep then I'll rock you to sleep...

...I have the rock.

Oh.

ALRIGHT, LADIES, IT'S AFTER MIDNIGHT, ALL THE KIDS ARE IN BED...

...IT'S TIME TO PUT THE LEAF BLOWER ON **HIGH!**

OOH! WHAT ARE **YOU** LADIES UP TO?

CONVENTION PHOTOGRAPHER

UH, SIR? I DON'T THINK YOU WANT TO BE HERE RIGHT NOW.

YES HE DOES!

THERE'S A BUG IN THIS ROOM.

TWITCH! TWITCH!

CHECK FOR CHILDREN!!

ALL CLEAR?

VROOM!

IF I WAS THAT WELL ENDOWED, THEN I'D WEAR A MINISKIRT TOO!

242

YOU MEAN YOU DIDN'T PUT THIS OUT FOR ME TO SIT ON?

BILLS

AW, LOOK AT THE POOR FROGGY.

CHRISTI!

DON'T WORRY, HE'S JUST A CLOTH FROG.

I'LL WASH HIM OFF AND CALL HIM **SQUISHY**.

LEFT!

RIGHT!

JEN? HOW WAS DRAGON CON?

BED.

246

BOO!

AAAH!

OH, WOW! THAT'S AN AWESOME MAKE UP JOB.

WHY THANK YOU.

MMM... DONUTS.

WHAT NOT TO SAY IN THE BEDROOM.

OH CRAP! OH CRAP! OH CRAP! OH CRAP! OH CRAP! OH CRAP! OH

OH CRAP. OH CRAP.

WAIT! I SMELL CHAINSAW.

WHAT ARE YOU TALKING ABOUT?

THERE'S A GUY WITH A CHAINSAW DOWN THERE.

NO THERE ISN'T.

I'M UP HERE!

AAAAAAAAAH!

PANT! PANT! PANT!

LET'S DO THAT AGAIN!

6♠

9♠

CLANG! CLANG! CLANG!!

WHAT ARE YOU DOING?

BENDING THE NEW WIRE SNAKE TO FIT INTO THE OLD HOLDER SO I CAN FIX THE SINK!

SO YOU'RE BREAKING THE NEW TOOL TO FIT INTO THE OLD ONE TO FIX THE BROKEN SINK?

WHY NOT JUST GET A HOLDER THAT FITS?

BECAUSE I HAVE THIS ONE!!

...YOUR LOGIC IS MIND BOGGLING.

WHAT NOT TO SAY IN THE BEDROOM.

DO YOU WANT TO HAVE A BABY?

OUT! OUT! OUT!

SST.

WHY DOES MY CAT LISTEN TO YOU AND NOT ME?

I BEAT HER.

WARP SPEED MR. SULU!

YOU MISSPELLED "BEAT."

WAIT, YOU MEAN THE BEET THAT YOU EAT DOESN'T HAVE "EAT" IN IT?

RIGHT.

BUT THE BEAT THAT YOU DON'T EAT HAS "EAT" IN IT?

YUP.

HOW DO THEY EXPECT US F*CKED PEOPLE TO LEARN THIS IF IT DOESN'T MAKE SENSE!

WHAT NOT TO SAY IN THE BEDROOM.

UH... JEN?

HEY, WILL! YOU'RE UP LATE.

YOU'RE ON YOUR WAY TO WORK, AREN'T YOU?

WELL, I GUESS THIS WILL FIT, BUT I KNOW HOW YOU LIKE A BIG, THICK KNOB.

HAPPYGOTH! DID YOUR HUSBAND JUST SAY **THICK KNOB**? YEAH, SEE?

NO! **NO!** I DON'T WANT TO SEE YOUR **BIG, THICK** KNOB! STOP WAVING IT IN MY **FACE!**

YOU'VE GOT A PROBLEM WITH MY **FENCING** SCABBARD?

YES.

YAY! MY BEDWARMER IS HERE.

I MEAN, MY **BOYFRIEND!**

HA, HA! THE CAT'S SITTING ON YOUR PILLOW.

WHAT?

EW! NO! OFF!

NOW I HAVE CAT BUTT COOTIES ON MY PILLOW.

YOU KNOW, ONE OF THESE DAYS SOMEONE'S GONNA FALL AND CRACK THEIR SKULL OPEN.

I'LL JUST HAVE TO FIGURE OUT WHAT TO TELL THE COPS AFTER I COLLECT YOUR LIFE INSURANCE.

LOVE YOU TOO.

YOU KNOW WHAT'S WRONG WITH THIS?

WHAT'S THAT?

YOU TRUST ME.

JUST BECAUSE I GOT MYSELF UP HERE, DOESN'T MEAN I KNOW HOW TO GET DOWN.

OOOH... LITTLE TO THE LEFT... ...MMMM, LOWER.

OH **YEAH!** THAT'S WHY I KEEP YOU AROUND—

...ER...I MEAN, ...I LOVE YOU HONEY?

YOU'RE LUCKY THAT YOU'RE CUTE.

YOU'VE BEEN DOING A LOT OF CUDDLY COMICS LATELY.

SORRY, WITH NO CONVENTIONS, YOU'RE ALL MY MATERIAL.

BUT DON'T WORRY, THANKSGIVING'S COMING UP...

...I'LL BE DOING CARTOONS ABOUT DEEP FRYING CHILDREN IN NO TIME!!

OOOH, I **HURT**!

NOTHIN' LIKE DEEP FRIED TATER TOTS AND CORN DOGS FOR DINNER.

WHAT DO YOU THINK ABOUT COFFEE AND ICE CREAM FOR DESSERT?

I THINK I'M GONNA START TAKING NOTES FOR THE CORONER'S REPORT.

NO, I THOUGHT THAT WAS **YOUR** HAND!

WHAT NOT TO SAY IN THE BEDROOM.

THANKS FOR DOING A RIDE-ALONG. I HOPE IT MAKES THE NOISE FOR YOU.

YEAH, ME TOO, THOUGH I DON'T USUALLY SEE A GIRL DRIVING A STICK.

I'M SURPRISED YOU CAN EVEN **DRIVE** ONE.

IT'S NOT **HEALTHY** TO PISS OFF THE DRIVER.

HEY GUYS, HAPPY—

HOLD THIS A MINUTE...

...COULD YOU TAKE OUT THE KITTY LITTER?

...THANKGIVING?

DID YOU BRING COOKIES?

AH, WILL YOU LOOK AT MY BOYS!

THIS ONE'S A FUTURE GARDENER...

...AND THIS ONE'S A FUTURE WINDOW WASHER!

WHAT? WHY ELSE WOULD YOU HAVE KIDS?

WEEE! YOU'RE FLYING!

UH OH.

OH, JEN? THE BOYS ARE TEETHING, SO THEY MAY BE A LITTLE DROOLY.

YOU DON'T SAY.

SIGH... I FINALY GOT THE BOYS PUT DOWN.

MRROW-

I WILL KILL YOU.

WHAT?

FAMOUS LAST WORDS.

OKAY, I GOT THE WIRE THING OFF OF IT.

NOW RINSE IT AND DIG OUT THE GIBLETS.

THE WHAT? **OH!**-

EW.

NPH!

MY **NOSE** ITCHES!

RUBBA! RUBBA! RUBBA!

NOW I CAN'T FEEL MY FACE.

265

Blood and Water by Jennie Breeden

FAMOUS LAST WORDS.

PITTER PATTER PITTER P

WHAT DO YOU WANT, EVIL ONE?

EEW! EEW!! HSSSSs

MOOOM IT TOUCHED ME AGAIN!!!

OK, I CAN DO THIS.

FEARLESS HUNTER! FEARLESS HUNTER!

OOKAY. TRY TALKING TO HER, THEN WE CAN UPGRADE TO THE BITING.

HOME DEPOT IS OPEN AT 4 AM, RIGHT?

FAMOUS LAST WORDS/WHAT NOT TO SAY IN THE BEDROOM.

VAL, HONEY, YOUR MOM AND I ARE GOING OUT TONIGHT.

SO YOU'RE RESPONSIBLE FOR THINGS HERE...

WHICH INCLUDES **THIS.**

AND DON'T JUST DROP HIM OFF AT THE MORGUE THIS TIME!

HSSS.

SNIFF SNIFF?

YOU HAVEN'T BEEN STASHING CORPSE'S FINGERS IN THERE **AGAIN,** HAVE YOU?!

BLURBLE

OH FOR THE LOVE OF ALL **THINGS EVIL!**

HOW LONG HAS THAT **TWINKIE** BEEN IN THERE!?

I'M COMFORTABLE. HOW CAN YOU NOT BE?

Page 1

LAN parties are creepy because you have 15 guys in your garage and an empty house.

Page 2

Yes, I LARP (live action role playing). I hunt down my friends in the woods with a padded stick. Sometimes nature gets in the way.

Page 3

I crap you not, he asked about hypnotists.

Page 4

I'm in the south. Once a month I get a guy in the comic shop who calls me "sugar" or "sweet heart" and I don't know why, but my stomach convulses. I want to yell at him, "Do you even KNOW me? How the hell do YOU know if I'm SWEET!?!"

Page 5

I usually have one-week stints where I exercise and then I'm over it for about eight months.

Page 6

The last panel the guy has his horseshoe upside-down, which is actually bad luck.

Page 7

I didn't actually get to say the storm trooper thing to the little brats.

Page 8

At Heroes Con, when I met the Pirate, I found out that there was a rumor that I was sleeping around. Suddenly I wanted to put a bag over my head and cut off any possibility of mistaken flirtation. I drove myself nuts until I realized that it's not my fault that a$$ holes can't tell the difference between being polite and flirting.

Page 9

I didn't actually hand out soap and sandwiches, but sometimes I wish someone would.

Page 10

My friend, Karl, shuffled through the con gnawing on raw meat and anyone who interacted with him. Later, he said that a couple girls hit on him when he was in the zombie makeup, which creeped him out. The girl is from a vampire comic that I did for Acrimony.org

Page 11

Pictures of the "Panties sale to Superman" can be found at devilspanties.keenspot.com/Dragoncon.html. There's also a picture of the two little grim reaper boys from the last panel.

Page 12

No matter how articulate I try to be, it just degenerates into "boobies". The evil Willow was a girl in a really good costume.

Page 13

I don't make this kind of stuff up. The pirate lady created the best Dragon Con drinking game ever!

Page 14

Agwa is florescent green.

Page 15

The pirates covered me in pink Sharpie. Some of it was hard to explain to Will.

Page 16

It wasn't until Ddragon con 2006 that I actually get the leaf blower, though.

Page 17

Clothes are replaceable. The books are my babies.

Page 18

Every time I see my sister she asks if I'm gay yet.

Page 19

The baby of the family has omnipotent guilt power.

Page 20

Yup, we went to Pegasus.

Page 21

I showed up a day early to visit my sister and found out after the class that the professor had planned a class around my visit to talk about webcomics.

Page 22

My sister pointed out that I had the comic equivalent of a reality show.

Page 23

It was weird. The parking garage was closed, but when I touched the gate it opened. I don't question good luck.

Page 24

Those one-dollar, vintage He-Man figures were awesome!

Page 25

I dressed up as Scary Godmother
www.jillthompsonart.com

Page 26

Watercolors make the BEST makeup.

Page 27

I used an orange, plastic pom-pom for my hair, and it came in handy.

Page 28
This holiday can't truly be appreciated without children.
Page 29
I got the breaking boarders idea from 9 Chickweed Lane.
Page 30
The only sport I've ever gone to watch...
Well, there was that one hockey game.
Page 31
My boyfriend's sister's husband's sister had twin boys, and we see them every Thanksgiving.
Page 32
I like to mess with babies, but I LOVE to give them back to their parents.
Page 33
When the grandmother saw that I had put the baby in the soup pot she ran to get her camera.
Page 34
Black Friday always weirds me out.
Page 35
They never make fun shoes in adult sizes.
Page 36
You know you're stuck when they make you be in the family Christmas photo.
Page 37
I swear, that's what she said; "you have baby now."
Page 38
Pixel has "cute" down to an art.
Page 39
I take no responsibility for the "mao" cartoon.
Page 40
My dad never did anything half way.
Page 41
Okay, they didn't put us in muzzles, but my brother did have a Klingon death match with stockings and turkey prongs. That's exactly what we wore to church too. The oldest boy is in red satin shirt and leopard print gloves.
Page 42
This is my mom's favorite Christmas cartoon. And that's exactly what I said when David Mack showed up.
Page 43
Okay, so I didn't actually lift my shirt, but I was thinking about it.
Page 44
Going salsa dancing with my siblings is a little

out of context, but I couldn't work it into a story ark so here it is out of left field.
Page 45
I had used my glasses from fifth grade for driving and only updated the prescription in 2006. Now I'm addicted to being able to see the leaves on the trees. But I'm not going to change my character design. Hell, I've got long hair, 5'6" and now wear glasses. I was never being very accurate anyway.
Page 46
I'm not talking about a mouse. My mom loved this cartoon, but my sister just said, "Ew."
I got Jehovah's Witnesses at the door and realized the fastest way to get rid of them was to simply say, "Yes".
Page 47
I went to What The Hell Convention at Goucher College. Four of the girls were wearing t-shirts that I had brought; Invader Zim, Labyrinth, and Batman. I almost thought they had raided my luggage.
Page 48
My favorite part of this convention is the Geek Auction. You buy one dance with the boy you're bidding on, and the guys sometimes get dressed up as themes. It's a lot of fun.
Page 49
I ended up buying a lot of guys.
Page 50
The girl at my knee is actually a guy.
Page 51
I got a lung infection after the con. I still drew the comic strip, but I used Sharpie. This was the birth of the Plague Monkey.
Page 52
I have a thing for Asian guys. The background images in the third strip are all covers to the mini comics that I did about high school and college, all of which are available on my website.
Page 53
Some sneezes are just orgasmic. The background pictures are snapshots of the magnets that I made with glass beads.
Page 54
Never ask an EMS guy how his day was. These cartoons were drawn about two years ago. I know McDonalds defeats the purpose of exercising, but it's really the only reason for

exercising in the first place.

Page 55

They were $30 Hot Topic boots. The soles fell off of them. My mom asked me what I wanted for my birthday and I told her New Rock boots. They're very expensive, but I figure it's about time to invest.

Page 56

It took two months to soften the leather enough to get my foot in, and a solid year before they stopped hurting, but they're worth it.

Page 57

Yeah, I'm not good at sports and don't pretend to be.

Page 58

Nigel just wanted someone to drive with him, but I slept through the drive. Later, Nigel told me just how close to death we came.

Page 59

It was a really slow convention.

Page 60

Yeah, I'm a total letch at conventions.

Page 61

The guys who don't have their toys anymore are the ones who enjoyed them the most.

Page 62

I'm not exaggerating, fourteen cats. The smell was pretty extreme.

Page 63

They had fourteen cats, two ferrets, a rabbit, and a horny toad.

Page 64

A friend of mine has one of these giant rabbits. They're terrifying. The's at least three feet long. She could eat my face!

Page 65

I believe cats have very deep, philosophical thoughts like the answer to life, the universe, and everything.

Page 66

It's a very odd moment when you realize that someone in a comic shop is actually wearing deodorant. You think I'm exaggerating.

Page 67

I swear, a sushi place had a "Little Nemo Special". I almost didn't get the cartoon done that day because "Dragon's Bones" was so damn good. I have a webcomic and yet the computer is a total mystery to me.

Page 68

I mow the lawn. I do a good job. But then I have to do it again the very next week! It's just not fair.

Page 69

LAN parties will always be an oddity to me. So much testosterone.

Page 70

I leave a hickey ONCE in three years and he'll never let me forget it.

Page 71

I wore those boots that one night, and then I had Steph take them, because I knew that some day I'd think it would be a good idea to wear them again, despite barely surviving the first time.

Page 72

It's amazing what we'll do to ourselves for a cat call.

Page 73

I love renting kids out so you have an excuse to do all the fun kid things.

Page 74

I can only have one bite of those deep fried Snickers bars. They're good, but just so damn sweet. I don't know how my sister can do it—those kids wear me out.

Page 75

I swear those instruments were rusty.

Page 76

Okay, I left the door unlocked ONCE! But good GOD, it had electrical tape holding on the headlights!

Page 77

I didn't actually get a Vespa, but I looked into it. I decided that the neighborhood between my home and work was just a little too sketchy for me to be driving a scooter through it at 11pm.

Page 78

Seriously, $20 was still in the glove box, but the painting on cardboard was gone. That was just too cool.

Page 79

It's amazing what Chinese takeout can do for a bad week. Actually, the car was stolen the week before the convention. They found it, but it was in the car prison for the weekend of the convention. Needles to say, I was a very stressed puppy during my weekend of sleeping in a parking lot with some pirates.

Page 80

I didn't realize I was going to Michigan. That's kinda north of Georgia.

Page 81

These were the girls from aworldlikemyown. com They saved me. And they're seriously that short!

Page 82

I found out that they were local and dropped hints that I wanted to sleep on their couch. Little hints like, "Can I sleep on your couch?"

Page 83

I had never been to a Red Robin before. You have no idea how much I needed that Bailey's milkshake.

Page 84

This clubbing adventure actually took place in Philly at the next convention. I seriously had to unwrap a girl in the bathroom.

Page 85

The guys were being so silly I had to do a cartoon about it… wait, was this at Heroes Con? It might have been. I combine a lot of the cons, so I don't have to do cartoons saying "I'm home," "Now I'm gone!"

Page 86

That's really how I met Seth Green. I gave up on trying to get on the signing list and on my way out the door, I literally ran into him. I then mowed down three five-year-olds to give him my book.

Page 87

Yes, I danced like a monkey the whole way out of the convention and he was walking right behind me as I did so. I have no shame.

Page 88

My sisters came to Heroes Con.

Page 89

I finally came to terms with my Amazonian baby sister being hot…Sorta.

Page 90

I didn't go to Vermont to have lunch with my two best friends. If I did, though, we had this virtual conversation. Apparently DJ is inseparable from her sidearm now.

Page 91

Yes, of course I shaved my toes. I don't want the pedicure people handling my hobbit feet. I'd much rather have them handle stubbly feet. I didn't let him give me a foot massage

because then he'd touch my legs, and those were stubbly. Yes, I'm a freak in many different ways.

Page 92

I catch up on all my daytime television when I'm at the mechanics. My car also breaks down a lot.

Page 93

The comics in the window are Wet Moon and Ultra, which were done by classmates of mine from Savannah College of Art and Design; Striip Tease, which is a web comic done by my old roommate; and Neato People, which is the comic that the characters from Strip Tease work on. The other two are Sheena and Invincible. I just threw those two in because I love Invincible and Sheena has boobies.

Page 94

Yes, I assault my boyfriend and his cat with my monkey slippers.

Page 95

I had to go to the party because I had a blue satin 1980's prom dress covered in bows and lace. Yes, the squirrels were using the pans as mirrors, and it turns out that the pears aren't the kind that you can eat anyway.

Page 96

Breaking the panels in the third strip is something that I saw done in 9 chickweed lane.

Page 97

I've got my own webpage and I still think writing code is like trying to hammer a square into a circle. The monkey ninja pirate was inevitable.

Page 98

I never draw Will reading a book, (because he doesn't) but reading his phone, instead. He has a whole library on the thing. It's weird. In college my housemate, Chris, would stay up all night working on his web comic, Stripteasecomic.com, and I'd ask him if he was just up or still up.

Page 99

Yes, I tried it once. Just once.

Page 100

Betty would really wear outfits like that. She could do the voice of Bobby's mom (Minnesota) on cue. It was creepy. The second strip was actually another co-worker who made the chocolate comment. The third strip happened word for word.

Page 101

Be afraid, be very afraid.

Page 102

Will got upset because the laptop that the fan sold me is better than his. I know next to nothing about technology and he's a tech geek.

Page 103

Arie's the artist of **www.aworldlikemyown.com.** She plays SCA and is just as bad with directions as I am.

Page 104

She also takes self defense.

Page 105

Most indie artists are very familiar with the midnight print run. Poor Arie was waaay too hung up on little things like cropping and having all the words on the flyer. I honestly thought it was a normal toy store that happened to be open at 1 AM

Page 106

It was my first time in a porn store. Dildos are illegal in Georgia, so our shops are kinda nasty. The ones up north are so pretty! The clerk had on a suit and showed me the Calvin and Hobbs tattoo he had on his arm.

Page 107

Carla Speed McNeil is my role model. She writes, draws, produces, prints, distributes, and advertises her own comic book; Finder. **www.lightspeedpress.com**

Page 108

I sat next to her for an hour before the guy came to take back his table, but not before I was interviewed by the Chicago Tribune.

Page 109

I don't know how to play video games. I'm pretty good at the first Mario Brothers. I played it when it first came out, and that's about it.

Page 110

I sat on a bench under the stairs at Dragon con handing out my card for three years. In 2006 the convention gave me a table... under the stairs.

Page 111

We played jelly bean Russian Roulette. Everyone takes one and we figure out who got the snot flavor by the look on their face.

Page 112

Characters found on this page are; Jessica Rabbit, Waldo, the Photo Gnome (he's an Atlanta thing). The Conan guy is a regular at Dragon con and the brunette is the husband who gave me the back rub. It wasn't until Dragon con 2006 that I actually got a leaf blower for the men in kilts.

Page 113

Bubba was supposed to have his own movie coming out, which is why he's wearing sun glasses; and the Pirate was supposed to have a part in the movie, which is why Bubba is standing in for him in these comics. I don't know what ever happened to the movie.

Page 114

Bubba's posing with two girls dressed as David Mack's Siamese twins from Kabuki.

Page 115

I don't make this stuff up.

Page 116

He was in standard porn positions; I just made up the part about the clamps and lube. IT's just the most random thing I could think of and I leave it up to the reader to make up the rest.

Page 117

There's a drum circle each night at Dragon con.

Page 118

That's Andy Lee in a David Mack "you don't know me" t-shirt. We never did find out if the couple in room 352 was arguing or having sex.

Page 119

The cat in all the strips is Pixel. She's a black cat, but that's a pain to draw, so she's usually just white. The customer seriously asked me this. I overheard the foreskin thing in Boston. I've blocked the rest of it out.

Page 120

I have a blurry camera phone picture of Darth Vader in my garage drilling.

Pages 121, 122

Will spent the whole week sitting in the beach house playing on his game boy.

Page 123

Aili's my redhead friend from first grade who got me into comics and drawing. DJ I met in middle school and she just gets more buff every time I see her.

Page 124

It took me three days to get used to DJ's boob size. She'd been a double D cup since middle school.

Page 125

I didn't make any of this up. Except the "what's in your pocket" happened in college when Lessa had me lay on the floor for a photo project.

Page 126

DJ's t-shirt says "breast inspector" and "I funked your girlfriend".

Page 127

We went to Toast in Boston and Christian Beranek from Silent Devil met us there and offered me a publishing contract.

Page 128

This was also the night that Lauren gave me my first sex toy. She was also the one who brought Christian to me, so she MUST be my fairy godmother.

Page 129

I took photos of DJ doing the Poi at the club for reference for these cartoons.

Page 130

I have a thing for effeminate, Asian men.

Page 131

DJ can only visit me in the winter so she doesn't get heat stroke, and I can only visit her in the summer so I don't freeze to death.

Page 132

I dress as Jill Thompson's Scary Godmother for Halloween each year: **www.jillthompsonart.com.**

Page 133

I only bake cookies once a year and that's for Thanksgiving. That's a lemon tree in their backyard that we make lemonade from for dinner. Gotta love Savannah.

Page 134

This was all word for word. Except the cat, I don't know what he was thinking.

Page 135

It was actually kind of hot that day, but I got so into wearing the scarf and hat and drinking hot chocolate that I forgot it wasn't cold.

Page 136

Lessa and Happy Goth went to the beach with me. We had fun being silly, They buried me in the sand and built boobs in the sand.

Page 137

Happy Goth had a kite shaped like a pirate ship. The only way to keep it up was to keep running.

Page 138

There was a kid next to us who wouldn't shut up. The girls gave me a mermaid body after we scared the kids with the "decapitated head on the beach" routine.

Page 139

Dolphins are great and all, but when you're in the "wilds" of the ocean and they get THAT close, then it's a bit creepy.

Page 140

The web comics cartoon was inevitable. We've all done it. Just one more strip and then bed, just one more, just…

Page 141

These strips were thought up while hiking with friend and his dog.

Page 142

I'm not a big animal person and some of the girls I've met are psycho. I don't know how anyone can put up with some of us girls.

Page 143

All too often we overlook the meaning or nature of something because it's all dressed up.

Page 144

This is as close to politics as I'll get with my comic strips. I just don't understand how people can still be prejudiced to gays and women and.. nope, I'm not getting political.

Page 145

I got a Jetta (it broke down three months later, and so I traded it in for my boyfriend's Scion). The flip key was the best part.

Page 146

It seems that everyone who grew up in the woods now have subdivisions over the next hill. My brother wore a leopard print, fuzzy, cowboy hat and matching gloves to Christmas Eve church service. We're Unitarians.

Page 147

My mom started the tradition of anatomically correct Christmas cookies. You should see her sand castles.

Page 148

After these strips, I got a sticker in the mail. It said "pigs are friends, not food". I grew up with pigs, they're fantastic pets. They're insanely smart. They're also delicious.

Page 149

When my brothers were 13 and 15 they were in Jamaica, and a bus hit the younger brother. As he lay there unconscious, my other brothers thoughts were "mom's gonna kill me." He came home with a band-aid on his chin and a great story. Later in life, this same brother broke his neck, flipped his truck twice, and likes to jump out of planes.

Page 150

Ever run down a hill and realize that you're just falling and barely keeping your feet under you? You know that you're an inch away from falling on your face. That's what doing a monthly comic book feels like.

Page 151

I'm industrious in the morning, but tend to slack off in the afternoon. Any time I go on a plane trip I end up watching CNN in the airport terminal. It's all apocalyptic news.

Page 152

Coffee makes me crazy.

Page 153

It drives me mad when people use "god bless" as a way of saying goodbye. They assume that you're the same relition. They'd go ape shit if someone told them to accept the goddess as their creator and savior.

Page 154

All these were conversations at What the Hell con in Guilford College… well, except for the vacuum thing.

Page 155

The fifth panel is Twinkie Bugs. Phillip, from Furmentation xodin.comicgenesis.com, makes them out of pez, pixie stixs, and a Twinkie.

Page 156

I was scared at first, but those college kids did amazing things with pinto beans and a microwave.

Page 157

He really is from Canada and they really had a section taped off for me.

Page 158

In the second comic strip the girls were howling like wolves (yes, those are supposed to be wolves) and I've got a jar of money with me. The monkey boy was so cute!

Page 159

I'm not making any of those conversations up.

Page 160

I honestly didn't know what a colonoscopy was, and I wish I never did find out. Apparently it's big in Japan. Without the scarves, then it's just not Harry Potter.

Page 161

That morning we were just talking about how gross it was that people were counting down until the Harry Potter girl was of age. Then these two guys, who were over 21, showed up dressed like that. Yes, I'm ashamed, but they were hot!

Page 162

The girl in the first panel talking does the comic agirlsandherfed.com The story of how indy got his scars was really good, but very long. I did ask Will before I did the hot Indy comics, and the guy's girlfriend e-mailed me to tell me she really liked them.

Page 163

Poor Will puts up with so much. Okay, so I drew one very big, detailed comic shop background and now, every time I draw the comic shop, I just paste in different parts of that background. It saves huge amounts of time.

Page 164

Yes, I was too tired to do a comic, so I did stick figures. This is one of my favorite comics that I've ever done. "My head is a giant egg" is a line from "The Animation Show".

Page 165

Yes, I still wear a retainer every other night. The guy beside us was really freaked out by how much fun we were having in those chairs.

Page 166

The Broad is an ex-girlfriend of Karl, who showed up as a zombie one dragon con.

Page 167

I had tape recorded the conversations at dinner that night to use for these comics, but couldn't for the life of me figure out what we were talkinga bout when The Broad delivered the two "you had to be there" lines.

Page 168

To this day, I will always rate the level of a night according to how much bail money is needed.

Page 169
I don't remember where I heard the "day pass" quote.
Page 170
Calling the cable company was one of the more infuriating twelve hours of my life.
Page 171
The tequila really did help.
Page 172
A co-worker really asked me this.
Page 173
I had forgotten all about going to the guy's party. I honestly couldn't remember being there. The sad thing is, I don't drink. I don't cook either. The smoke alarm goes off before the oven timer. Our third housemate has shown up in the comic all of two times in the three years that he's lived with us. He's quiet.
Page 174
This one might be a bit too much information, but my gynecologist had his eyes dilated. How can I NOT do a comic about that? And I was frustrated over calendar choices.
Page 175
My Fairy Godmother/editor hangs out with the hottest comic guys in the industry. I've also been meaning to do a comic for a long time where she takes that wig off. She never wears it anymore. Plus, it's a pain in the butt to draw. Somehow, during that weekend, Andy Lee mentioned that the ultimate love was tauntaun love. A tauntaun is that thing in Star Wars that Hans shoves Luke into to keep him warm. Andy's a strange, strange man.
Page 176
I got that jelly stuff all over my lap too. There's a picture of Nigel begging for the rum devilspanties.keenspot.com/mega06.html
Page 177
Found porn is when you find a toy that was not meant to be pornographic, but is very much so. Just like the vibrating teletubbies.
Page 178
The guy that bought me sushi was also at Dragon con lamenting the lack of Parfait with the Conan looking dude.
Page 179
To this day, I have yet to get someone who is dressed as Darth Vader to say, "I'm a pretty, pretty princes".

Page 180
Strawberry lemonade is the tastiest stuff ever.
Page 181
Anime cons are usually packed with little girls in very skimpy costumes. As a result, there are also some creepy guys lurking about. Some friends and I decided there should be a "conscience rental service". The Conscience would be a big burly man who would walk around with the little jailbait girls. Most conventions you try and fit as many people as possible in one hotel room (because the glamorous life of a comic artist doesn't pay much) and there's usually beer involved.
Page 182
When my sister saw David Mack she told me that she didn't see why I kept going on about him. Then she went to talk to him and he gave her one of his dazzling smiles and crossed his fabulous arms and she couldn't remember what she had meant to say to him.
Page 183
www.girlswithslingshots.com is a fantastic comic. The creator, Danielle Corsetto, can say the most shocking things with the cutest giggle.
Page 184
My neck hurt that entire weekend. A friend did some terrifying contortion things to me, and it did feel better. But mostly I felt fear.
Page 185
My baby sister is fabulously silly.
Page 186
Summer can belch at will. She told me about how she had started dancing to some music one booth was playing. Other people started dancing too. One man yelled to her if fries came with her shake, but it was the rather large gentleman next to her who answered.
Page 187
Mike found me at a later convention and said that he thought this cartoon was funny.
Page 188
My mother DROVE the short bus.
Page 189
Of all the people in my family, the baby is the most outgoing.
Page 190
The first strip is out of an exact conversation.

When one of the babies rolled over you could see part of its leg or arm. Really really creepy.

Page 191
They had a Snoopy theme for the room. The paintings in the comic are pictures of what I did on the wall. The second panel is Starry Night with Snoopy.

Page 192
We take a very leisurely attitude towards out mountain walks.

Page 193
Crowds were forming to watch the deer on the mountain in Georgia, but at my family's house in Virginia, we have to honk at them to get them out of the way on our drive down the driveway.

Page 194
He made deep fried sausage. It was heavenly.

Page 195
The pictures in the background are of our second cat who passed away, my Darth Vader helmet, and the batman utility belt that I got for my birthday.

Page 196
It's fun having your own reality to mess with.

Page 197
Actually, the grandmother said that at the dinner table. The Intern told us about it later.

Page 198
Christi did do her version of this conversation on her webcomic **www.inthedpuddle.com**

Page 199
That's how Nigel and I greet each other. What's a little groping between friends?

Page 200
The dangly bits conversation took place outside of a convention party in Philly.

Page 201
That's how Nigel picked up a long time girlfriend.

Page 202
I thanked them for the Mountain Dew, but saved the Red Bull for later.

Page 203
I honestly have no idea what that girl was talking about.

Page 204
Kevin Smith had stopped by the hotel bar at one of the cons, but had to leave because he was quickly getting mobbed.

Page 205
Heroes con, 2004 was the first convention that I had a table at. I hadn't sold a single comic yet, and that's when I heard of Gravy Boy.

Page 206
At What The Hell con, run by Guilford College in North Carolina, the artists of Gravy Boy and I decided that we should be each other's nemesis. Ever since then, they cover my table with their books every time I leave it unguarded and I throw pixy sticks at them.

Page 207
I did trip over a long box while chasing one of the Gravy Boy creators back to my booth when he saw that I wasn't guarding it.

Page 208
I kept going back to check on the boots.

Page 209
Roller derby is very fun. The girls are tomboys and great friends with each other, but will tear apart other teams of women.

Page 210
That's exactly what the little blond girl said to me.

Page 211
Going to the bathroom in roller skates was the most terrifying experience of my life.

Page 212
I'll wait until Will's done, and then finish his meal. He hates it when I do this because he says it makes him look cheep.

Page 213
I've chased after fire flies all my life. I've never thought of it this way until Will pointed it out.

Pages 214, 215
This is word for word how Will got his car.

Pages 216, 217
I loved my old Neanderthal Cell phone. It was indestructible. But my flying monkey can record cartoon ideas and take reference pictures and keeps my convention schedule. Unfortunately, it also sometimes decides that it doesn't feel like doing what I ask it to.

Page 218
Will really did go on about how technologically advanced the phone was and then began to play solitaire on it.

Page 219

Ironically enough, this comic strip went up the day the Pinky and the Brain DVD came out.

Page 220

The second Pirates of the Caribbean had just come out.

Page 221

His accent was Scottish and made me melt.

Page 222

This was at Connecticon 2006

Page 223

The guy who won the auction asked me to put his brother in the comic strip instead of himself.

Page 224

I got to share a booth with Sluggy at San Diego Con. He had a PILE of plushies. They were soooo soft.

Page 225

Will said that if the house was burning down and it came down to me, the cat, and his car, he said that the car would be outside already, I could get out on my own, and he'd grab the cat.

Page 226

The framed artwork in the background is the cover art to other DP books.

Page 227

I get super stupid when I geek out. These strips are from San Diego con of 2006.. I got to share a booth with Sluggy, Partially clips, Super Frat, and Fragile Gravity.

Page 228

Whenever there's a guy with one of those circle with the bar across it shirts, that's Chris Daily from **www.stripteasecomic. com.** He overheard the conversation of the man on the cell phone and when I posted this cartoon, I got an e-mail saying it was something from a video game. That scares me.

Page 229

Every time I try to show my high tech phone off to someone, it breaks.

Page 230

Based on my "convention humanitarian" strip, someone dressed as a pirate and handed out soap at DragonCon.

Page 231

The women I was sharing a hotel room with introduced me to Bailey's in coffee.

Page 232

We were in the hallway between Artist Alley and the dealer's room at Dragon con. It was a prime traffic spot. In the background of the second strip you can see where the "real" artist alley is.

Page 233

One of the women who I was staying with overheard this on an elevator. No, that's not my pirate. He's just one of many Jack Sparrow costumes at Dragon Con. He even had a jar of sand from the second movie.

Page 234

I've been doing cartoons about it for years, but Dragon con 2006 was the first time that I actually went out and got a cordless, battery operated leaf blower and really did go Kilt Hunting. There's a calendar. It's on my website store.

Page 235

My thighs hurt the next day and I didn't know why. Though, that's not uncommon for Dragon con.

Page 236

One of these days we're going to have a fairy game hunt at Dragon con.

Page 237

I really do fan girl all over my fans.

Page 238

This woman is seriously 6'3" and has an L cup. Her boyfriend is hot. She has trouble with fan girls sniffing around after him, though.

Page 239

In panel one can you find; Storm trooper, storm trooper pimp, barbarian, flaming carrot, overweight trekkie, Waldo, a fairy, and a geisha? There's also Eon Flux, Cowboy Bebop, Cutter, Screamer, Sims girl, and gothic ball couple; but those aren't as recognizable.

Page 240

I just love my stick men. The one guy's eye is getting bigger and bigger.

Page 241

Gravyboy had a really hard time getting into the convention. They're my nemesis. They blamed me. In the background of the second to last panel Christi has found the Spaghetti Monster.

Page 242

It doesn't take much to get Blue Beards kilt up.

Page 243
The contact Drinking didn't happen to me, I was just told the story.
Page 244
Christi did find a squashed toy frog in the parking lot.
Page 245
I didn't punch the Haunted House worker, but I have worked in houses and known people who have gotten hit. I was close though. If you get in my face and scare me, my natural reaction is to defend myself. I got an angry letter from a Haunted House worker saying that it wasn't funny.
Page 246
The house we went to was Nether World in Atlanta. It was SO cool and detailed and so much work went into the decoration. I wanted to go back through with the lights on just so I could admire the art.
Page 247
It was actually Happy Goth who got separated from our group and was clinging to a random guy the whole time.
Page 248
Some of the monsters would chase me and I'd yell, "oh crap, oh crap" and they'd yell it too while they chased me.
Page 249
Lessa really did smell the chainsaw before we saw it. When he jumped down behind us she dragged me down the hall so fast I was bouncing off the walls.
Page 250
This little girl actually said that. And she was in the best Batgirl outfit too. My reply was "Well, I can't say I miss him."
Pages 251-253
I spent a solid week working on that sink.
Page 254
Life makes no sense.
Page 255
This is a story Aaron told me at a convention. The newspaper reporters got to the scene and the headline that printed the next day was "Jesus and Death were walking down the street at 3am".
Page 256
Happy Goth and her husband really do fence.
Page 257
The cat belongs to Will. I'm ambivalent to all animals.
Page 258
We play the leaning game.
Page 259
I think human beings are compelled to have companions so that someone can get those hard to reach places on our backs.
Page 260
Deep fried food sends me into a coma. Will has a deep fryer.
Page 261
Will's sister had twin boys.
Page 262
It's not Thanksgiving without a deep fried critter.
Page 263
I have a confession… I'm a sucker for kids. I just like to give them back too.
Page 264
Will's sister's cat meows really loud.
Page 265
Happy Goth's husband used to do a week long geek scavenger hunt in college. They'd do things like build a working wind mill or solve huge math problems. He'd also played with power tools after four days of no sleep.
Page 266
I did a vampire comic for an online magazine. These are the comics.
Page 267
Another "Famous Last Words" from the geek scavenger hunt. He had five car batteries connected to a wire, and I think he might have touched it at one point.
Page 268
I like putting the vampire family portraits in the background.
Page 269
The pictures on the wall are of literary vampires. One is an actual portrait of Vlad the Impaler and another is a snapshot of the Munsters.
Page 270
I keep a battle axe with my umbrella by the door too. There's a family picture in the background with Val as a preschool dork.
Page 271
I did some sketches for a creepy uncle, but he never showed up.

WHO SAID WHAT?

WELL DONE!

I FUNKED YOUR GIRLFRIEND.

I DON'T DO "CUTE".

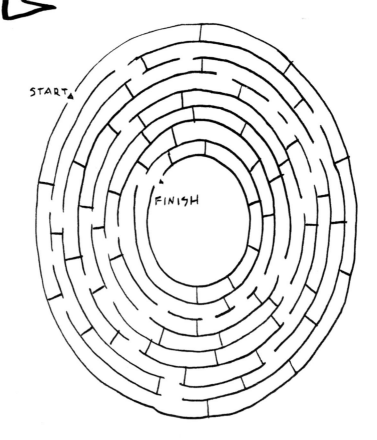

MLAFE OTBSO   _ _ _ _ _   _ _ _ _ _

OI NOVC NNTE   _ _ _ _ _ _ _ _ _

LVEIDS NPAITSE   _ _ _ _ _ _   _ _ _ _ _ _

GLUEAP KOYMNE   _ _ _ _ _ _   _ _ _ _ _ _

RETIAP   _ _ _ _ _ _

MATCH UNSCRAMBLED WORDS WITH IMAGE

287

WHICH IS THE SAME..?

— — — — — — — — — — — — — —
1 2 3 4 5 6 1 7 8 9 10 11 12 12

AHDRT DAVER

— — — — — — — —
    7   2

ELMAF OTBOS

— — — — — — — — — —
       11   12

LAELBT KRSIT

— — — — — — — — —
             3 4

TIUYITL LBTE

— — — — — — — —
  8   6   5

NPKI

— — —
1 9

NEFAICFE

— — — — — — — —
10

MATCH THE CHARACTER TO THEIR LOGO

289

ANSWERS

Extra Flame

UNSCRAMBLE

PRETTY PRINCESS
1 2 3 4 5 6   1 7 8 9 10 11 12 12

DARTH VADER
7   2

FLAME BOOTS
11   12

BALLET SKIRT
3 4

UTILITY BELT
8   6   5

PINK
1   9

CAFFEINE
10

MATCH THE CHARACTER TO THEIR LOGO

MATCH THE PERSON TO THEIR CLOSE UP

WHO SAID WHAT?

 WELL DONE!

I DON'T DO "CUTE".

I FUNKED YOUR GIRLFRIEND.

MATCH UNSCRAMBLED WORDS WITH IMAGE

MLAFE OTBSO _ _ _ _ _ _ _ _ _ _

OINOVCNNTE _ _ _ _ _ _ _ _ _ _

RETIAP _ _ _ _ _ _

GLUEAP KOYMNE _ _ _ _ _ _ _ _ _ _ _ _

LVEIDS NPAITSE _ _ _ _ _ _ _ _ _ _ _

ABOUT THE AUTHOR:

By day, she's a comic shop register monkey and by night she's a raving lunatic with a webcomic. That's what you get when you have a degree from Savannah College of Art and Design in Sequential Art (comic books). Graduates from art college usually begin their careers with food service or retail. Knowing this, Jennie Breeden began a webcomic so that she could retain some shred of art in her daily life (that, and she wanted fanmail). She resides in Atlanta and terrorizes the customers of the local comic shop and schemes her next attack against her rival: her boyfriend's cat.